TO MY PUPILS

Contents

Illustrations

All photographs are by Pamela Booth, F.R.P.S.

Acknowledgements

When the continued demand for this book, a quarter of a century after its first publication, led the publishers to decide on the production of a revised and up-to-date edition, I was delighted but a little overawed that Victor Booth's daughters should invite me to undertake the task. Without their help and encouragement, and active co-operation in the preparation of the biographical introduction by their search through family records, it could never have been completed.

I am also indebted to the many others who helped in many varied ways. From her own experience as a composer and as professor at the Royal Academy of Music, Margaret Hubicki gave me inestimable help, and will never know how our discussion aided and clarified my ideas. For information on Victor's own early days at the Academy, I have drawn on the reminiscences of Dame Irene Scharrer, Mr and Mrs Harold Craxton, and Mr and Mrs Vivian Langrish. My friend and colleague, Muriel Holland, gave valuable help and advice, and discussion with Ethel Scarlott and Phyllis Hards threw light on the views of those outside the music profession.

Letters received from Victor's former pupils were both helpful and a touching reminder of the wonderful work he did at the Academy. All remembered his courtesy, encouragement, and unfailing patience, as well as the practical help he gave them. My own students, past and present, also contributed many useful suggestions, especially as to simplicity of approach. I extend my warmest thanks to them all, for their support made my work on this book a labour of love.

Finally, I am grateful to my cousins, Joan and Joyce Fagg,

and Frances and Harold Hey, whose hospitality ensured welcome quiet in which to work at weekends; to Carol Price, who typed the manuscript; to Bernard Fillery who read through and ˅corrected the text, and to Louise Helms.

Preface to the Revised Edition

Without doubt this revised edition of *We Piano Teachers* will make many new friends, ever widening the circle of those who have cause to be deeply grateful to Victor Booth.

From its first publication in 1946, the book's helpful guidance on the fundamental principles of teaching has, amongst teachers and students alike, gained world-wide recognition for the wisdom and discerning musical sensibility that it contains. In it Victor Booth stated his convictions simply and frankly, writing with sincerity of purpose and breadth of vision.

In the Preface of the first edition Sir Stanley Marchant, who was at that time Principal of the Royal Academy of Music, wrote: '. . . (this) book is an epitome of a life's work and has that ring of authority which only long experience and a mature mind can give.

'Students who have reached a high degree of proficiency as performers are often surprisingly nonplussed when they begin to teach. They are seldom able to recall the various stages of their own development: they find it difficult to think in simple terms, and to realise that as teachers their approach to the subject must be from the pupil's standpoint.

'Primarily, it is to these that Victor Booth's book will bring inspiration, but everybody concerned with the study of pianoforte playing will find the book of absorbing interest and great practical value.'

To bring certain aspects of the book up-to-date, Adele Franklin, who, like myself, studied with Victor Booth at the R.A.M., has revised it—making any necessary modifications in such a way that, most fittingly, they have in no sense disturbed the essence of the original text. It remains the testimony of a highly sensitive artist and inspired teacher whose charm of personality and unfailing kindness made Victor Booth much beloved . . . Overseas as here in Britain.

MARGARET HUBICKI

Royal Academy of Music, London.

Biographical Note on Victor Booth

Believing that those who read and profit by this book will want to know something of its author, I have ventured to add this biographical note, since the standard reference books supply little information.

Victor Booth came from New Zealand. His father, Joseph Booth, who is described on Victor's birth certificate as having been a 'General Agent', was a Yorkshireman and had been born at Northoram in 1836. Joseph emigrated to New Zealand's South Island, and there at Timaru in 1877 he married an Australian girl, Susanna Jones. Twenty years younger than her husband, she had been born at Geelong in Victoria in 1856, and was gay, social and popular. The couple's first son, Harold, was eventually to be killed in early manhood in the South African War; their second was Victor George Booth —the future pianist, composer and singer—who was born on 4th November 1880 at Oamaru, a coastal town just south of Timaru.

The brothers lost their father while they were still both very young, and their widowed mother, who had a considerable talent for music, supported them by teaching the pianoforte. They were educated at Waitaki High School in Wellington, and here Victor's musical ability was soon noted. He had already received some training from his mother, and now studied the piano under A. J. Barth, and singing under Miss Amy Murphy. He did credit to their tuition by achieving the highest marks of any New Zealand student in the Trinity College, London, examinations of 1895, and it was eventually decided that he should go to study at the Royal Academy of Music in London.

Before leaving New Zealand on this great adventure, the

young musician was honoured by a farewell concert in his home town, both his tutors at Waitaki High School travelling there to play and sing on this occasion. The yellowing cutting that survives from the *Oamaru Echo* of that date conjures up the scene.

The Mayor having unfortunately been called away to Dunedin, the Chairman of the Committee took his place in performing the necessary little ceremony in the interval. 'The name of Booth', the Chairman was reported as saying, 'had been associated with music in Oamaru for very many years —long before he himself came to the place. One of his most pleasurable memories was his association with Victor Booth's mother in some of the finest musical productions ever given in Oamaru. It must have been extremely gratifying to that lady to see such a demonstration of kindly feeling towards her son and such a testimony to his musical abilities and personal popularity.

'In 1895 Mr Booth was at the top of the list in the Trinity College musical examination for practical work, gaining 95 per cent of marks. The examinations of the College were held all over the Empire, and only five candidates had obtained that high percentage, Mr Victor Booth being the only one in New Zealand who did so. He was now qualified to obtain higher honours in the realm of music and was about to leave for the Old Country to seek them.

'He now desired first to present to Mr Booth as a memento of the occasion the Programme printed in gold on satin, which would remind him in London of his friends in Oamaru. He had also to present to him a very small but useful token, in the shape of a purse of sovereigns, of the esteem in which he was personally held in Oamaru and of admiration of his musical abilities.

'The second part of the programme was then proceeded with, and when the concert was finally brought to a close with the National Anthem: three cheers were called for Mr Booth and the call was responded to right heartily.'

One can imagine that the fond mother's heart was indeed gratified, and since she lived until 1940—later making a second marriage—she must also have rejoiced in her son's later success.

Victor entered the Royal Academy of Music in 1903 and

studied the piano under Carlo Albanesi, whose daughter was the famous actress Meggie Albanesi. He found him a congenial teacher, always speaking in most affectionate terms of this brilliant musician, and made excellent progress. In 1904 he won, among other awards, the Charles Mortimer Prize and Bronze Medal for singing and piano; gained his Siver Medal in 1905, and in 1907 won the Westlake Memorial Prize and the MacFarren Gold Medal—the latter being one of the Academy's highest awards to pianists.

Among his fellow students was Clara Bennett Smith. She, too, came from a family with a musical tradition—organ builders were among her ancestors—and she herself was a fine singer. She was a pupil of Sir George Henschel, whose methods Victor often praised to his own pupils, and had been awarded the Sainton Dolby and Melba prizes. Soon they married and in 1914 twin daughters were born to them, Pamela and Patricia. The girls were gifted in the visual, rather than in the musical arts: Patricia—under her married name of Morley—was to become known as a painter, and Pamela—who retained her maiden name for professional purposes—as a photographer, her skill being shown in the illustrations to this book. The vein of music, however, has been re-opened in the next generation. Patricia has a daughter, Margaret, who trained at the Royal Academy of Music as a pianist and has undoubtedly inherited Victor's gifts as a teacher, and a son, David, who was a chorister at St George's Choir School, Windsor Castle, being a member of the choir at Princess Margaret's wedding, and later singing the treble solo at Bristol Cathedral for the Clifton School Centenary service. Pamela's daughter, Shauna, is also musical and has a reputation as a flautist, although her son, Bayntun, reflects her own gifts and is a student of photography at the Regent Street Polytechnic.

From being a student at the Academy, Victor Booth graduated to the teaching staff, becoming Professor of Pianoforte and eventually a fellow. He had inherited the charm and popularity of his mother, and Dame Irene Scharrer remembers vividly the handsome young fellow student with his perfect piano technique. He was particularly fond of the music of Schumann, Brahms and Rachmaninoff, and his own compositions, individual though they are, have a romantic touch

B

which links them with what he most admired. Unfortunately, his teaching commitments absorbed more and more of his time and he wrote comparatively little. One brief composition, inspired by the sound of his daughters' baby feet outside the music-room and called 'Little Footsteps Outside the Door', was played by Dame Myra Hess (godmother to Pamela's daughter, Shauna) on one of her American tours with great success. His songs, which have a pure delicacy of feeling, were sung by such great artists as Carmen Hill and Elena Gerhardt.

Victor excelled in the lecture-room as in private tuition, bringing the same friendly intimacy and simplicity of approach to the larger audience. To convey some idea of what these lectures were like, I have included the note outline of one of them in this book as an appendix. As his reputation grew, so came the demand that he write a book, in order that more students than could ever work with him personally might share in the help he so inimitably gave. *We Piano Teachers* was published in 1946, was immediately successful, and went into successive impressions.

Always of delicate health, Victor suffered from chest complaints which were aggravated by the English winter, but it was with a sense of great shock that his students and friends received the news of his death on 21st September 1948. I had myself studied with him and remember very well the sense of loss I felt, and the regret that no more students would open the door of the music-room to find that tweed-suited figure seated at the piano awaiting their arrival, and trying over on the keyboard in harmony with his own clear tenor perhaps the very phrases which had caused them difficulty on the occasion of their last lesson. How kindly was his welcoming smile, and the familiar inquiry, 'Isn't this where we went wrong?' and somehow the difficult passage was difficult no longer.

The memorial service was held on 21st October at Marylebone Parish Church, opposite the Academy where he had studied and worked for so many years. There remains, for those who did not know him personally, this book, and if I have assisted in giving it a renewed lease of life in the altered circumstances of the modern world, I can think of nothing that would please Victor more than to be a continuing help to others.   A.F.

Introduction

To have studied this book in the great detail which has been necessary for its revision has been in the nature of reliving my piano lessons with Victor Booth at the Royal Academy of Music. As such the experience for me, and later for my students, has been invaluable. The latter on their part have been of the greatest assistance in their comments and appreciation.

If there is one thing that stands out from the many letters I have received from former students of Victor Booth, it is that good teaching is timeless. All speak of his unfailing patience and courtesy, as well as his remarkable ability to put them at their ease. That so many of Victor's past pupils are now distinguished composers or concert artists, while others are engaged in doing splendid work in teaching and carrying out the precepts laid down in this book, is evidence of his skill and inspiration.

The personality and character of the teacher are the pillars upon which good teaching is built, and it is these qualities that will be impressed upon the student for his or her future life. If but one quality were required by both teacher and taught it would surely be perseverance. This fundamental requisite implies courage, patience, enthusiasm and tenacity of purpose to keep the torch burning brightly. All these Victor Booth had in abundance.

Recently I was looking through some papers, when I found the following notes written by Victor Booth immediately before I took my Diploma Examination, and I am sure that no better introduction could be found.

Let the master speak for himself:

The Approach to Touch

I. *Exercises in preparation for Touch*

Preliminary To warm hands clench hard and very tightly, but gradually, to a slow count of eight. Open as far as possible to similar count. Upper arm to be free. Gradually reduce count to 1. Then open and shut hand quickly.

(a) *Shoulders*
Stretch arms straight overhead and with hands locked raise each shoulder alternately, standing perfectly erect.

(b) *Arms*
(1) Raise and bend in line with shoulder and and twist backwards and forwards from relaxed to tense positions.
(2) Raise forearm only for similar movement.

(c) *Wrist*
Move hands slowly up and down to fullest extent, pausing at end of each movement. Later, practise octaves thus with the utmost relaxation.

(d) *Fingers*
(1) At keyboard, stretch each finger laterally with the next (including the thumb) to fullest entent; particularly 3 and 4.
(2) Raise and hold with other hand each finger in turn as high as possible above the remainder, and with arm relaxed, proceed to depress keys with remaining fingers. Include thumb.

II. *Mental attitude to Touch*

(a) *Cultivate a feeling of awe of* the Instrument, thinking of the artistry of its construction, its delicacy, and the possibilities of beauty of sound it holds.

(b) *Cultivate the spirit of humility* and receptivity, as in the presence of the great composer, whose work you are about to endeavour to interpret.

(c) *Keep always relaxed*, holding particularly the upper arm buoyant and balanced.

(d) *Play with the fingers,* except for cantabile, when the weight
of the arm should be allowed to come through.
(e) *Feel the moment of sound*
(f) *Never play past the sound*
(g) *Play over the keys* to encourage lighter touch.
(h) *Listen* to your own playing
(i) Be your own *conductor* as you play.

In revising I have amended only where alteration was
essential, and where I have added material, it has been only
after careful consideration of what Victor himself might have
approved. The headings for the chapters, for example, which
are new to this edition, were gleaned from the rough notebooks
he kept from 1924, and which were lent me by his daughters to
help in the preparation of this book. Material which is solely
mine, except for the quoted passages, and which comprises the
biographical note, this introduction, and the bibliography, is
marked by my name or initials.

Together with the notebooks mentioned above, we were
fortunate enough to find the notes for Victor's lecture 'Musical
Sense allied to possible effects in performance,' and since I was
able to include in this introduction Victor's advice on the best
initial approach to playing the piano, it seemed most fitting
that the book should close with the words of that lecture, given
in 1927, and which contains the kernel of his musical thought.
It has not been possible to restore with certainty what Victor
intended to give as musical examples in every case, although I
have been able to do so in some instances. These, and the music
examples given elsewhere in the book, were of the greatest
assistance to his students when they could be heard, and it is
to be hoped that a recording of these may eventually be made
available.

ADELE FRANKLIN

Woodcote, Oxon, and
Wimbledon, S.W.19

I

We Piano Teachers

The vital principle in the pursuit of knowledge is to enable the pupil rightly to instruct himself—so from what follows let us extract our store of maxims.

'Teachers, like poets, are born, not made' is a statement true in only one sense. Natural endowment, although essential, must be regarded merely as suitable soil in which to plant the seed. When the plant begins to grow it needs perpetual care and attention if we would eventually bring forth the finest blooms. To succeed as teachers we must possess an unfailing interest in the subject of Music; make an unceasing effort to understand cause and effect in all we do and hear done; and go on from day to day drawing fresh knowledge from every available source.

Intending teachers should fully appreciate that the craft of teaching cannot be learned without experience, and that probably more is learnt from our failures than our successes. Teaching others to do step by step what we can do more or less completely (having forgotten the steps) is usually our position when, having graduated as performers, we wish to begin teaching. Teaching others how to do what we are able to do ourselves is not so simple as it sounds.

For instance, many of our best teachers have been fine performers. It is also true that any first-class performer may eventually become a first-class teacher, yet results prove that this is not necessarily so. The chief interest of the performer very naturally centres in his own performance. But every teacher's interest must centre in that of the pupil. There is, therefore, hope for all those teachers who try hard enough. For there are numerous instances in which indifferent as well as good performers are doing yeoman service as teachers.

It is reasonable to suppose that a performer who might give helpful advice on the interpretation of a Beethoven Concerto would feel somewhat at a loss if called upon to give a lesson to a comparative beginner. By this I mean that although we may know the end perfectly, as performers, do we, as teachers, know the gradual means of getting there? Much which prevails in the final stage of performance has necessarily become sub-conscious and automatic, even although it was originally learnt very consciously bit by bit. If we performers wish to train others as we have been trained, the problem is, how much of the step-by-step process can we remember, or re-learn, if we have forgotten?

It is true that the craft of teaching cannot be learned except by practising it. Yet, listening to lectures and reading about it have a distinct value. In this way we become possessed of definite ideas which enable us to make a satisfactory beginning, and these should help us in our further development. We can learn only by the two types of experience: our own and that of other people. In this latter way many facts can be learned in a short time that might otherwise take ages to accumulate.

Although it is desirable that our individual research should begin as soon as possible, we are bound to graft this on to what might be called the common stock of accepted knowledge.

Of necessity, teachers are divided into different classes. The type and state of efficiency of the pupil generally determine which class we work in. From the beginner to the advanced performer there are many. It has been my privilege to co-operate with many teachers in their early teaching days, and to be present during many lessons given both in and out of the examination room. From these experiences I can testify that the usual deficiency in these early attempts at teaching is an entire absence of method in dealing with the correction of faults.

One of the reasons for this would seem to be that the would-be teacher fails to appreciate how complicated for the beginner is the playing of even the easiest piece of music. Every such piece presents several difficulties, and each of these must be tackled separately. If we lack experience our immediate need is to discover some plan of procedure, and this is most impor-tant; for only by studying the approved methods of the teaching of others can we hope to learn how to begin to employ method in our own.

Teachers will know what I mean when I say that on one day we seem to have real vision, and on another not an idea worthy of the name. But surely this affects only that elusive quality called 'feeling'. We must remember there is always, even on our worst days, a right and wrong way of teaching the several elements which form the foundations of our work. Without, first of all, careful attention to these, artistic finish, our ultimate aim, is impossible.

It is essential to know primarily exactly what each element is. The next stage is to deal with each one separately. To attempt to deal with several simultaneously is to court failure. Doing 'one thing at a time' is the only sure way to success.

Principles which guide teachers in general education apply equally to the teaching of music. We must realise, however, that although it is necessary to generalise in order to memorise our knowledge, this method is useless to a pupil unless we explain the particulars upon which any generalisation is based. In interpretation, by all means, let the pupil have the whole, but we must explain the parts. In other words, it is not sufficient to perform a piece in its entirety; we must also explain each effect in detail; the relationship of phrase, as well as the general character of the piece; why one part is more essential than another, and give the reasons why this accent or that gradation is of greater importance than others. Pupils learn with much more zest and interest that of which they can see and hear the bearing and the use, and thereby they eventually learn the process of building up an artistic whole and working independently.

Knowledge begins by understanding: yet it is of little value without recollection. Once the understanding has been established, we must demand from the pupil recollection. All learning is memory in some form or other. The student should be encouraged to make a real effort of attention, which is indispensable to remembering. We must be sure to drive home this fact.

Usually, what is hastily acquired is hastily lost, therefore never be in a hurry for results. Cramming is of little permanent value to anyone, as in the case of verbatim learning of questions and answers for examinations. Real knowledge exists only when it has been honestly acquired and made a subconscious instrument for effect. Then the seed will have germinated, even though in time it has become unrecognisable or seems to have disappeared altogether. An instance of this lies in the learning of fingering and note groups in quick passages, when the very conscious, slow, early efforts of associating certain fingers with certain notes eventually merges into the subconscious muscular actions of final rapid performance.

All thought begins with sense impressions. Musical thought is no exception to this rule. In the teaching of Time, the mind is largely trained by our physical sense of regular movements. When this knowledge has become fixed in the mind we are then, and only then, able to use it in our musical thinking. Musical performance demands the turning of thought into action. Just as an artist must carefully observe every aspect of an object before drawing it, so the pianist must imagine every detail within the musical phrase before performing it. This imagining demands the co-ordination of several musical concepts which gradually ripen in the mind and produce mentally the fruits of the composer's creation.

'There comes a moment, say, in the learning of a language, when the hearer catches its spirit, receives a new idea through its means, and actually uses it as an instrument of thought.' We must all have experienced this extraordinary change in learning any Music we have really mastered. When, having spelt out each detail in laborious repetition, we suddenly seem to grasp the musical message intended; when the fingers become the servants of the mind; when they begin to respond sub-consciously; when the mood is able to control the entire situation.

There are those who can use Music in this way almost from the beginning. They are the lucky ones—the musically endowed. But every pupil, of whatever ability, must eventually find the way on to this subconscious road if the results are to be musical. The more the fingers do become the servants of the mind, the more immediate the subconscious response, the better the enjoyment of it.

Musical knowledge becomes an instrument of thought only when all the memory exercises have served their purpose; when the conscious detailed work which probably seemed dry and uninteresting has merged into the subconscious; when every musical concept combines and is controlled by the main musical mood or idea. Not until then.

2

Earliest Stages

*Some knowledge of the laws which govern all mental
development is essential for all teachers.*

'One thing at a time', is perhaps the most important axiom
in teaching or learning anything.

What is the one thing we must teach 'now' is always the
question!

For instance, the beginner who wishes to read and play an
easy piece is faced with three primary difficulties. The music
has to be read, the notes found by certain fingers, and finally
played in time. Until these can be used in combination, no
so-called tune can even be recognised.

Such expressive details as legato, staccato, variety of tone,
accent, phrasing and correct tempo must all wait, although
they, too, must ultimately receive individual attention.

After deciding exactly just what we are going to teach, the
next question is, what is the best method for teaching it? If our
method is right we shall be able to rivet the pupil's attention on
each individual problem to be solved and remembered. Otherwise we shall certainly find the pupil's attention wandering.
Obviously the closer the attention the quicker the solution, and
the more certain the remembering.

In order to enable us to put our finger exactly on the weak
spots, let us consider first the nature and number of the particular senses engaged when tackling our various difficulties.

I make out the number to be six. Seeing, hearing, feeling
(muscular), time, shape and mood. What we want to know is
the particular part played by each. The last three are, strictly
speaking, not senses. But we talk about a time sense and a
feeling for shape and mood, so I feel justified in including
them under the main heading of 'Senses', for purposes of
convenience.

The Eye

The eye is responsible for reading the written page—the only link between composer and performer. It brings all signs and symbols to the understanding. It also helps to guide the hands and fingers about the keyboard. And here it might be as well to frame this axiom, which should be memorised: 'It is not enough to notice and understand the signs and symbols; in addition, their meaning must be brought to the imagination'. Every pupil must be taught early the significance of these three ways of regarding the written page: to notice, to understand and to imagine the music.

Many faults can be traced to indifferent observation.

The Ear

Broadly speaking, the ear is employed in two ways. Listening to other people's performances and listening to our own. In the first case the music will impress each of us differently according not only to our development and concentration but also whether we are or are not what is called 'musical'—sympathetic to the emotional appeal of music, in other words. Listening to our own playing is another proposition altogether. This is a major difficulty right from the beginning, and its development can never be said to be complete, however old we get. Every teacher is in duty bound to cultivate this side to the utmost in every pupil. Many faults can be traced to an almost complete absence of this faculty and a tape recorder can be invaluable.

The Muscles

It is through the muscular sense that we become aware of the various physical sensations which accompany our actions and reactions when playing the piano. It tells us how it feels to make different sorts of sounds at different speeds. How it feels to prolong, to connect, to stop sounds, and enables us to develop what is called a keyboard sense.

It is only through this sense that we can trace the why and the wherefore of technique.

Time

The time sense not only enables us to register the actual moment when each sound shall begin and cease, but regulates the pace of the music and gives us control over regular movement. To be of any practical value it must have become a mental picture, although it can only be learned through physical channels. This sense is dealt with fully in the next chapter.

Shape and Form

In its initial stage, shape and form in music are analogous to a feeling for punctuation in any language. It is responsible for the recognition and comparison of all group forms. It is best acquired in the first instance by our being taught how to listen to the performance of others.

Mood

The sixth and last is the mood sense. This implies a proper imaginative treatment of all groups in their mutual relations, both rhythmically and tonally, in accordance with the spirit of the music. The interpretation of the music is embodied in all signs and symbols denoting the intentions of the composer. Finally an instinctive feeling for just the right 'tempo'. This last is perhaps the most important function of the mood sense.

When reading music at the piano, all these senses should work together either consciously or subconsciously. When faults arise, what we teachers have to discover is which sense works badly or not at all. Then we shall be in a position to deal with the cause of the trouble and to rivet the pupil's attention in the right quarter.

As an example, suppose we wish to teach a short legato passage. The pupil plays this badly with wrong fingering and disconnected sounds. Singing the passage in question is usually very beneficial and helps largely to correct this very common fault. Occasionally this way is not possible, as sometimes even those very musically endowed have great difficulty in singing correctly. In this case an alternative is to get it performed by either a woodwind player or a good violinist. Legato is more easily explained and understood when one breath, or one bow, can encompass a phrase or part of a phrase. This makes a good starting point and will naturally lead to the analysis of the original faults which we decide were caused by poor efforts of the eye, ear and touch because:

(1) The fingering has not been observed.
(2) There has been no concentration on listening to effect produced by connecting the sounds; or
(3) There has been no capacity developed for doing this.

So we have to deal with three faults instead of one, and these can be tackled in any order, provided they are dealt with separately.

The faulty listening and the bad fingering can be put right much more easily than the touch. It will be best to deal with these first, proving by our own examples what is right and what is wrong. In the case of the touch fault, the pupil must be taught the gentle art (and it must be gentle to begin with) of 'Walking' on the fingers. We must point out that one finger has to give way as another one begins to do the work.

The measure of our success as teachers depends very largely upon our ability to use this sense-analysis intelligently.

There are four different ways whereby we teachers can help our pupils to acquire musical knowledge and store the memory with necessary facts:

(1) By our example in performance
(2) By explanation of the various musical effects
(3) By developing the habit of self-tuition in the pupil
(4) By setting suitable tasks, musical and technical, according to each pupil's capacity. (Correct choice of studies.)

If we give a close study to each of these headings we can discover the lines along which our development as teachers will run.

It is essential to realise that the living voice is the most potent influence in inspiring pupils in every type of education. Only thus can be created that subtle and indefinable sympathy so desirable between teacher and taught. Our demonstration performances must be viewed from this angle. It is most important to appreciate that these should be well done, and are worth working for. The better the example we give, the greater the possibility of establishing high ideals in the mind of the pupil, setting a higher standard of what to listen for during performance.

But we can't leave it at example alone—that would be expecting too much. Our little lecture must be delivered both before and after each performance. We do this by drawing attention to, and giving reasons for, each musical effect in detail. This kind of work demands considerable patience and facility of explanation on the part of the teacher. So we are bound to regard this and example in performance as two of the main essentials in every teacher's equipment. Only thus can we indicate to the pupil how to think musically when working unaided.

It is true that pupils do not come to us for what may be called self-tuition, but for help and guidance. Nevertheless, our aim must be to make them ultimately independent. We begin to do this almost in the very beginning. As each scrap of knowledge becomes absorbed the pupil is taught how to use it when alone.

It is a good rule never to tell them anything we can make them tell us, and never to do for them what they could do for themselves. As they develop, it becomes more and more important to show them how to use the knowledge they should already possess. There are always three questions they should ask themselves: 'What have I got to do?' 'Have I succeeded in doing it?' If not, 'How should it be done?'

In the early stages we are, of course, bound to be more or less dictators, getting results mainly by example. We say, 'Do this', 'Do that', 'This is right', 'That is wrong'. The exact nature of the explanation given will naturally depend on the age and intelligence of the pupil. From the beginning, however, we must work by gradual progress towards the independent use of all accumulated knowledge. There is something wrong with the teacher's method if the pupil always expects to be told. To illustrate this point. Supposing we play through a short piece to a pupil who has had the necessary previous training. Any of these questions might be asked: 'Where do you consider is the end of this phrase?' 'Where is the loudest point?' 'What is the length of this note on paper?' 'How long should it last?' 'Do I give it enough length in sound?' 'What is the meaning of crescendo?' 'Do I make a good one?' 'Which is the greater crescendo in this series?' And so on ad infinitum.

There are two definitely different methods always used in teaching: (1) If the pupil has no previous knowledge, we supply it by 'telling'. (2) If the knowledge ought to be there, we endeavour to extract it by 'questioning'. It is only when the second method can be applied independently that the pupil is able to work efficiently alone.

As well as choosing the right type of music, the detailed tasks used in learning it must be set by the teacher. These consist of explaining in detail what has to be done and how it is to be practised. Showing pupils how to practise is the major part of music teaching. It is the great burden which lies heavily upon every teacher, and herein we find ample opportunity for originality of treatment.

A definite plan of procedure is essential both in choosing music and stating the tasks to be overcome. The steps must be carefully arranged and the repertoire graded. Only in this way will the musical ladder gradually be climbed to the top. Every rung should have its place in the ascending scheme.

Much of the value of the Associated Board and similar examinations lies in the fact that the plan of work has been designed by admitted leaders in the teaching world. All the material has been carefully chosen and each succeeding grade made a step forward from its predecessor. Whether these examinations are taken or not, much can be learned by a close study of the requirements contained in the syllabus. This is often the shortest cut when looking for the right type of piece for any pupil.

Here are three very simple conditions of homework to be given in the early stages: (1) Never too much. (2) Something very definite which admits of easy correction. (3) If possible, such as admits of only one way of being right. In other words, let us keep to the simple things of which the pupil, without assistance, can say whether they are right or wrong.

Broadly speaking, in teaching we give advice from two points of view: (1) Work preparatory to the next lesson, suggesting what has to be done in preparation; and (2) work supplementary to the last lesson, adding something to what has already been said and pointing out where the pupil has failed in preparation work.

Matters of fact, such as fingering, notes, time and duration, should be acquired by the pupil alone, yet, alas, too often we take for granted that this has been done when it has not. We have not only to see that it is done once correctly, during the lesson, but to have the patience to hear it over and over again, before we can expect good habits of work to become ingrained. It is only by our repeated efforts at each lesson that we can train a pupil in a similar way to endeavour to rectify errors when alone.

It is inconceivable in these days of broadcasts and gramophone reproductions that any beginner has not already heard a great deal of music before attempting to learn the piano. What we have to discover is how much can the pupil apprehend and recognise of those musical elements which he is about to learn to use in his own performance. A few questions must be asked in order to discover the pupil's disposition towards music generally, and the nature of the impressions made by music already heard.

C

3
Time in Music

The metric must come before the rhythm

In discussing Time in Music we are bound to use a large number of terms. Some of these can be very confusing to a pupil. 'Time', 'in Time', 'out of Time', 'Tempo', and most of all 'Rhythm', all need defining.

It is generally accepted that the word 'Time' stands for two things: regular pulsation of beats, and the grouping of these into bars by regularly recurring accents. Music is said to be 'in Time' when all the notes are placed in exact relation to a consistent and regular pulse. 'Out of Time' when the pulse is irregular or inconsistent. 'Tempo' applies only to a particular pace or speed.

The text-books tell us that 'Music consists of melody, harmony and rhythm'. But as music, for the listener, exists only in performance, with rhythm as the vitalising and controlling factor, we venture to modify this definition, thus putting rhythm in its right perspective.

So we say 'Music is rhythm featured by melody and harmony'. In other words, the melodic and harmonic groups in written music, although indicating rhythmic shape, depend upon rhythmic movement to bring them to musical life.

It is difficult to find a short comprehensive definition of rhythm. Here are two, giving different aspects of it: 'Movement to and from points of crisis' (McEwen); 'The systematic grouping of notes with regard to duration' (Grove).

A more simple and direct definition combining the significance of each of these seems necessary, so we venture yet another: 'Rhythm is regularity in movement, accent and design'. The term 'rhythm' is thus used to embody all that is included in the term 'time' but to this must be added 'balance' in pattern, or design. With this meaning, it is expressed in groups of one and one, two and two, or more, beats or bars.

These balancing groups form what is called a 'phrase'. In performance they are welded together into one continuous rhythmic curve, by using what has been called 'one span of attention'.

When teaching time, always begin with regular pulsation. Just as in life itself, so also in music, the regular pulse-throb is the evidence of living force. Without this vitalising foundation, accuracy of notes and all the varieties of tone and touch fall short in their meaning.

Some teachers, who do excellent work when dealing with the written theory of time, seem quite unable to teach a pupil how to play in time. Unless we ourselves possess a sense of time, it is quite obvious we cannot expect to develop it in others. To play in time means to realise and control regular movements at any given pace. So that is our present teaching problem.

We begin by educating the mental side through the physical, making use of those senses which enable us to feel, see and hear. Response must be to movements made. For instance, in walking or running, those made by us, we feel; those made by others, we see; and the sound of the tread in each case, we hear.

To be of any practical value for purposes of playing the piano, this comprehension of movement must be conjured up by the imagination and used by it. Without this mental rudder no performance can be steered with any rhythmic certainty into any cadential harbour.

Creating a time sense, where this is lacking, is a very difficult teaching problem. It means developing ability to imagine and measure movement mentally. Time in music might therefore be said to be measurement in space.

The passing of musical time is measured by what we call 'beats'. But every beat fulfils two functions. Not only that of position but also that of length. We must become aware of the length of time taken between the beats. In this way is created not only our sense of movement but also that of pace. So in our teaching we must make clear the following facts:

(1) At the exact moment when one beat ends another begins.
(2) Every first beat is not complete until we begin the second.
(3) Nor is the second ended until the entry of the third.
(4) No one bar is completed until the moment the next begins.

The realisation of time measurement is hindered, and not helped, by our musical notation. Unfortunately, wide gaps in the printing prevail. These are all against the mental comprehension of continuity in movement.

Having discussed position and length in regard to individual beats, we must now explain the difference in quality between successive beats. In this relation a clear understanding is essential of the term 'accent', and of those twin rhythmical terms 'weak' and 'strong'.

'A sound is said to be accented when it attracts the attention of the hearer in virtue of some quality or characteristic which distinguishes it from its neighbouring sounds.'

For most people the term 'accent' means only loudness, or tonal stress; but it can be and must also be used rhythmically. Then 'it is applied to a sound which attracts attention in virtue of its position in time'. In this way 'it makes itself felt as an underlining of the musical punctuation' (McEwen).

Inherent in that of accent lies the meaning of the terms 'weak' and 'strong'. These are the twin rhythmical pegs upon which we hang every musical unit. The quality that makes one accentuated and the other not, determines which is which.

The beat which initiates movement, preceding the accent, is termed 'weak', and that which indicates its culminating point and bears the accent is 'strong'.

In 'two in a bar' accent occurs on the first of the bar.

In 'three in a bar' it can occur on any of the three beats.

In 'four in a bar' it can occur on either the first or third beats. This rule takes no account of syncopated accent. When a bar begins on a strong beat, the preceding weak beat, although not indicated, is implied.

In teaching these musical facts it is best to draw some analogy.

The tonal stress or accent can be explained by words with weak and strong syllables such as 'Today', 'Tomorrow', etc.

The movement, to that of a gymnast swinging 'from one horizontal bar "to" another'. If the movement is to be made successfully his thought must be directed to the 'finish' of his swing.

Or it can be explained by the trajectory or movement made by a stone which is thrown to hit some object. The mind is directed 'to' the object.

'Look ahead' is the advice to give.

In music the rhythmical unit is always felt as one thought—as unchecked movement towards accent and away from it. It is like incoming waves which break before going out; energy running in to a point, then energy running out again. In this relation some explanation of masculine and feminine endings is necessary.

One way to begin teaching the apprehension of 'length' in time is to compare a bar in music with a straight line. Draw a short line and explain the similarities.

(1)   That the length of either lies within two terminal points.

(2)   That it takes an additional point, that is three points, to divide the line into two equal parts.

(3)   Four points to divide it into three, and so on.

Substitute the word 'beat' for 'line' and 'notes' for 'points' and we see the similarity.

This analogy will help to prove the fact that no beat is complete until the entry of its next-door neighbour. One point in time means nothing. There must be at least two to measure and create movement.

Before the pupil attempts to play anything we must test and awaken the rhythmic sense. This we do by demonstrating with simple well-known tunes with two or three beats in each bar. Our example must be played in strict time and the accents on the first of each bar exaggerated.

We draw attention to three things: (1) the regular pulsation, (2) the pace, and (3) the accents. Then follows the usual plan. Tell the pupil to clap or tap, imitating the rhythm of our example, taking care that the clapping is even.

In this way the pupil learns to feel, see and hear pulsation physically; incidentally, the hands and arms make movements similar, if exaggerated, to those used when playing.

We now suggest four simple exercises, which turn the theory of time into practice. They exemplify most of the points already discussed. But they can only be regarded as a beginning. No time names should be mentioned until Exercise 3, and then only when we add 'sound' duration to that of time. Each exercise must be introduced by our own example repeated several times. Use should be made of the imitative method. The pupil thus learns what to do by careful listening.

Exercise 1 deals with the one note only, indicating one point in time. The pupil is to learn to make single sounds at any given moment.

The procedure is: we count sharply, one, two, three, four—for two or three bars. While we go on counting, the pupil is told to 'play a note' on one particular beat and to play it again each time this beat recurs in our counting.

Instruct the pupil to listen carefully to the pace, so as to get the sound at the precise moment it is due.

The movement of the hammer must be timed to strike the string at this precise moment. This is usually referred to as 'Timing the Key'. It certainly provides the first peg in musical progression.

Exercise 2 deals with two notes, indicating two points in time.

We proceed as before. This time the pupil is told to play notes on two adjacent beats; either on one, two; on three, four; or on four one. We, of course, count the full four beats for several bars. Now make the following points clear:

(1) That these notes not only indicate beat places.
(2) They also measure the length from one beat to the next, thus initiating movement and pace.
(3) When the notes are played on four, one, this is an example of movement progressing from a weak 'beat' to a strong 'beat'.

Exercise 3 deals with three notes, indicating three points in Time.

If we use two crotchets followed by a minim, two bars of 2/4 time, we get an arresting pattern 2/4

It is an easy unit for the ear to recognise and remember.

The repetitions should be made with some variety in notes and intervals. Point out that this rhythmical unit is an example of progression from a weak 'bar' to a strong 'bar'.

Up to now, having only discussed time lengths, we must now introduce sound lengths. 'Duration', as it is called.

Explain the working of the damper and that we get duration by holding the key down for the length of any written note, and letting it come up when its time value is finished.

Play the unit used in Exercise 3 only once, but go on counting for another bar. Then point out, the sound of the minim ends exactly at the entry of bar 3.

Every note that we play, with the single exception of the shortest staccato, requires some degree of sound duration or 'tenuto', as we say. The importance of this simple lesson cannot be over-stated.

Exercise 4 deals with four notes, indicating four points in time.

We use three crotchets and a dotted minim.

The process and explanation are similar to those in Exercise 3.

These exercises merely point the way. Every variety of rhythmic pattern can and should be dealt with in a similar manner!—The metronome can be of great assistance in the preceding exercises for home practice.

Any ensemble work such as duet playing (using either one or two pianos) is usually beneficial in correcting rhythmic weaknesses—in fact all ensemble work, chamber *and* orchestral, is of inestimable value in building up a rhythmic sense. In these days of excellent school orchestras, it is usually fairly easy to find companions for the former type of activity. Encourage your students to work along these lines. It will improve their knowledge of the repertoires of other than their own instrument, and great will be their reward—and yours!

We now make suggestions for dealing with some common time faults:

(1) To correct the misplacing of a dotted note, tied note, or syncopation:

Begin by substituting a sound for the dot, tie or syncopation. Then leave out the sound, but keep its time place well in mind. This method should get the proper place and length of the dot, tie or syncopation and correctly place the note following.* For instance, in 6/8.

first play

and repeat often enough.

Then play as written with the tie. It is important to note the position of the accents in the two examples.

(2) Misplacing of 'in-between' syllables should always be corrected in this way.

Supply notes for every sub-division in the group. Then leave out all but the written notes. For instance, in this example

first play and repeat several times

then play as written :

The second and third semi-quaver places will exist in the

* In Bk. 1 *Mikrokosmos*, Bartók suggests a tap of the foot should be substituted for the held note. (A.F.)

mind so the dotted note gets its proper length and the semi-quaver and the note following their proper places.

Usually pupils do not play 'out of time' when the movement is of regular groups continuously supplied by either hand. The moment, however, that dotted and longer notes are introduced into what was a regular moving series, we must look out for trouble. The reason for this, in most cases, is mental. Pupils fail to supply in the imagination the measurement of the values which divide the beat, or the introduction of the varied time values upsets their sense of regular pulsation. This must always be watched.

(3) Combining different time groups in the same, or different hands.

This always creates serious difficulty. Some pupils go down to the grave never having learned to do this. The best way to tackle it is, as always, first to establish the sense of regular pulsation by clapping or tapping. Then imitate this pulse movement and play only those sounds occurring at beat places. Now add the notes of the sub-divisions in each hand or each part separately. Keep the pulse movement going all the time. Finally, play the hands or the parts together.

Repeat this process over and over again at every lesson until the pupil has learnt the trick of it.

As an example: suppose we wish to play two in the time of three—two notes in one hand, three in another.

If the tempo is slow enough this combination can be learned

from a single line rhythm

We say

and bring in the second note of the quaver coupled with the 'and'.

But at a rapid tempo we must work differently. Point out the necessity of first bringing in the automatic feeling induced by repetition of the group which must include the following pulse point. This should first be developed in each hand separately.

It may be necessary to repeat over and over again, until the automatic feeling is fixed. Then, keeping the same pulse going continuously, play the hands (or parts) together.

In teaching three in the time of four, or four in the time of five, etc., this is the only method which will give satisfactory results. It is the patience and perseverence with the formula in many repetitions that yields success.

(4) Inconsistency of tempo can again be explained only by the lack of any standard of regular pulsation in the mind of the player.

It is always a mental fault. Put the mind right and then we can regulate and control the tempo between adjacent contrasted sections.

(5) Uneven groups of notes. Hurrying all the notes on to the last of the written group, making this the longest note.

(6) 'Hands apart' is another time fault.

This may have a physical basis but it is probably an aural one. 'Listen attentively' is the cure, as a rule.

However, with some pupils the fault is so habitual that we have to produce some exercise which can be practised when alone.

Try 'tapping' with both hands together on the table.

First with the left before the right then with the right before the left, finally make both taps synchronise.

When doing this exercise, make slight movements with both arms as well as hands. This will exaggerate the necessary 'physical' habit. Incidentally, a correct muscular co-operation is thus being educated.

I suggest that before giving the lesson it would be helpful to meditate on all possible time faults a pupil might be expected to make in any particular piece. Side by side with this list devise some method for dealing with each separate fault. Working in this way we soon accumulate a list of valuable exercises. The use of these will relieve much tension and many a trying situation.

When observing the lessons given by student-teachers during various examinations, I have noticed that although they were able to detect the faults in time, they had no plan or method for the correction of them. Correction as well as detection must be practised.

Always remember the principle involved: 'There is no effect without a cause'.

Our business is to probe for causes.

4
Technique

Our task is to provide the right kind of facts prepared in the right manner and in correct order.

It is unlikely that anything new can be written concerning the underlying principles of technique. These have been so fully dealt with by such experienced teacher-writers as William Mason in America and Tobias Matthay in Britain, as well as by other writers both here and abroad, that I can lay claim to no new discoveries.

What one can do is to concentrate on the minimum of essentials and possibly throw some fresh light on the teaching of these.

In my earliest recollection the only advice I remember receiving from my piano teacher was 'Lift your fingers'.

This slogan pursued me even after I went to study farther afield. Still the same instruction: 'Lift your fingers'.

A good deal of my practice time, in those days, was spent in repeating various technical exercises. When practising, this perpetual finger 'lifting' gave me considerable pain in the forearm, but I was informed that was proof positive that I was developing my muscles in the right and proper way. It showed that I was working well and that eventually I should work through the pain and come out on the other side with strength and endurance.

So I plodded on hopefully, more or less unhappily, and without much success.

Although my hand was large, I had considerable webbing between the fingers. No notice had been taken of this, and that my finger lifting was therefore bound to be restricted. It could never be high.

A high-stepping finger action was the pride and evident joy of both my early masters; but they were the happy possessors of hands free from webbing.

This, no doubt, explained their own freedom of action in lifting the fingers high.

When it came to octave playing the advice was the same. 'Lift your hand'.

I was told to extend it to the span of an octave and practise ample up-and-down movements from the wrist. However much I practised in this way, I found it impossible to play octaves even reasonably fast without tiring painfully.

Perhaps my memory is bad, but I don't remember ever being told to 'relax' anything. A gathering despair threatened to terminate my pianistic efforts, until one happy day (I suppose somebody must have given me the idea) I tried playing octaves in a new way.

With all my fingers lying on the key surfaces, keeping the wrist loose and gently swinging the forearm, I proceeded to play repeated octaves up and down the piano. First in groups of eight, then four, three and two. Finally I played a scale.

All the while I kept contact with the keys (Pl. I).

I found the up-and-down forearm movement a completely comfortable one, where the up-and-down hand movement from the wrist had been most uncomfortable.

This was the beginning of what might be called the regeneration of my technique.

Armed with the watchwords of comfort, ease and freedom, I found that the mists of despair were gradually dissipated and I began to see things more clearly, and really make progress.

It may seem strange to begin a chapter on pianoforte technique with this rather long personal reminiscence, but the twin discoveries of key contact and a freely swinging forearm were the turning point in my development, and I feel it might reasonably prove the same 'open sesame' for others.

So many books have been written, and so many pages filled, with the most confusing and conflicting ideas on the subject of piano playing, that any teacher who reads widely is almost bound to be bewildered.

Young teachers who have got into complete muddles very naturally ask to have their ideas straightened out and simplified. They use book words, the inner meaning of which they don't understand. They are, indeed, full of the theory of technique but completely vague about how to turn this into practical essentials.

This chapter is an attempt to sift some of the wheat from the chaff.

As our aim must always be to make the fingers the servants of the mind, let us never forget that the mind is the controlling factor. The mind must be trained to know just what the fingers intend to do.

Most of us know how to begin operations.

We first show the pupil the instrument (the frame, strings and sounding board), then the mechanism for playing it. But it is just here where we can go wrong in our explanations.

The sympathetic action of the key, the hammer and the damper must be 'proved'. The influence of each upon (1) how sound is made, (2) how it continues and (3) how it ceases must be demonstrated.

It is important to stress the fact that the key is a see-saw lever. The end we see and use, goes down. The other end which we can't see goes up. It is the other unseen end which operates the mechanism for making and stopping sounds. (It helps to imagine the hammers as mechanical fingers working in exact reverse to our own).

Experiments should at once be made to demonstrate the following facts:

(1) That sound is made by 'down' key-movement. This lifts the damper and causes the hammer stroke on the strings. The sound-making stroke is instantly followed by a slight rebound of the hammer.

(2) That sound continues (the string vibrating in diminuendo as it always does) only so long as the damper remains up and the key remains down.

(3) That sound is stopped by 'up' key-movement. This allows the damper to fall on the string and the hammer to resume its place ready for action.

These are the only facts that should be introduced to begin with. Later on, by more experiment, the pupil will learn further facts:

(4) That sound begins when the key is 'nearly' down.

(5) That it ceases when the key is 'nearly' up.

(6) That any additional pressure after the sound is made

and the key is down can't affect the sound, because the hammer is out of action.

(7) That the quicker the 'down' key-movement, the quicker the hammer stroke and the louder the sound. The more slowly the key is depressed, the softer the sound.

Still later on, the action of the pedal levers will need explanation.

And that is all the pupil need know about the piano as an instrument.

When we come to deal with how best to play the piano, matters are not so simple.

Judged by all the literature on the subject, pianoforte technique is a tremendous business. So that when we try to simplify matters, we venture on a path where many 'angels have feared to tread'.

The physiological reasons for this and that activity may be very interesting to quasi-scientific experts, but we teachers will be wise to content ourselves with as little physiology as possible, and confine ourselves to simple statements.

When should the wrist be loose and when held?

What is the difference in sensation between one that is held and one that is stiff?

What does a free elbow feel like?

These are the kind of questions to which we need answers.

Different teachers produce similar and often excellent results by entirely different methods. The following suggested method need not be regarded as the only one.

The important thing is that we have some plan that will enable us to develop a pupil's technique, and always along comfortable lines.

When playing the piano either loudly of softly we are bound to use what is called 'combined touch'. The finger, hand and arm muscles are inextricably bound up with each other, and it is not desirable (even if possible) to implicate one without the other.

Freedom means sympathetic action by all.

Even if we confine ourselves to the statement 'Play with the fingers' (and it is perfectly true every sound must be made by finger action), it is only possible to get this done successfully if there is combined sympathetic action from shoulder to finger-tip. The finger-tip is the only actual physical contact we have with the key. It needs to be extraordinarily sensitive, and its connection with the rest of the hand and arm analysed as much as possible.

In all these exercises the relative length of the student's arm should be studied and the stool height needs to be carefully adjusted to help get the 'feel' of them.

Certain terms are bound to be in constant use when discussing touch problems. Such are:

    'condition and movement',
    'exertion and relaxation',
    'momentary and continuous',
    'action and reaction'.

It is necessary to think of these in pairs if their significance is to be understood. Knowledge of their exact meaning is essential when explaining any muscular activities.

It is also important to know whether they are unseen and merely felt as 'condition' or whether they are obvious as 'movements'.

Both condition and movement can be induced either by exertion or by relaxation. And both of these can be either momentary or continuous in use.

For all actions downwards there will be points of reaction upwards and these can only be at the knuckles, wrist, elbow or shoulder joints. We must know how these points are affected (whether in a passive or active way) if we are to supply force in the right manner.

Now we come to the four main essentials for a good technique:

(1)   The balanced arm (Pl. II*a*)
(2)   The hollow hand (Pl. II*b*)
(3)   Comfortable finger movements
(4)   Forearm freedom.

Each of these requires detailed explanation:

(1) The general condition of the arm is one of continuous balance, poise or support (Pl. II*a*).

It is induced by shoulder muscles which contract and hold the arm in the playing position.

The feeling for this condition of balance can be learned by resting the five finger-tips on the tops of the keys and by moving the hand and forearm up and down the keyboard horizontally.

Plate I *The position of the hands*

Plate IIa
The balanced arm

Plate IIb
The hollow hand

Plate IIc
*The wrist on top
of the keys*

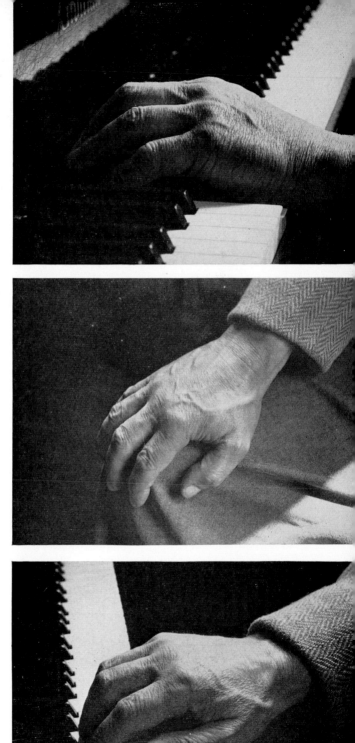

Plate IIIa
The wrist on the bottom of the keys

Plate IIIb
The cupped hand

Plate IIIc
The normal position

Plate IVa
Dropping the fingers

Plate IVb
The normal position

Plate IVc
Dropping the fingers

Plate Va *The clapping exercise: up*

Plate Vb *The clapping exercise: down*

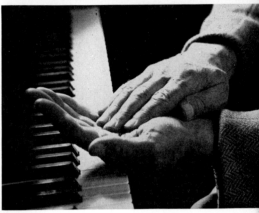

Plate Vc *The same: with single finger up*

Plate Vd *The same: with single finger down*

Plate VIa *The 3rd finger as pivot*

Plate VIb *the 4th finger plays*

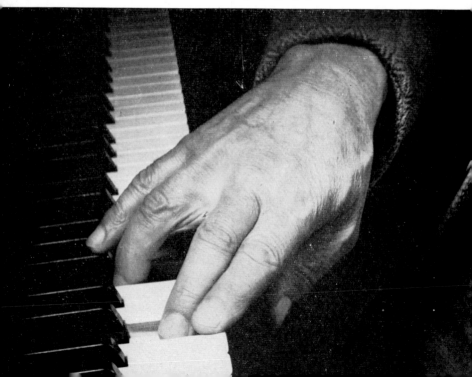

Plate VIIa
Finger drill:
1, lift

Plate VIIb
Finger drill:
2, drop; and 4,
cease

Plate VIIc
Finger drill:
3, press

Lent TERM 1936.

Thursday Pupils		1st HALF						2nd HALF						Time of Lesson
STUDY	Pupil's Signature	1	2	3	4	5	6	7	8	9	10	11	12	
	Barbara Lee	·	·	·	·	·	·	A	A	·	·			✓ 9.30
	Carroll Vincent	·	A	·	·	·	·	·	·	·				✓ 10
	Doreen Chillingworth	A	·	·	·		·	·	·	·				✓ 10.30
	Gwen Ricthe	·		·	·	A	·	·	·	·				✓ 11
	Jean Mackie	·		·	·		·	·	·	·	·	·		✓ 11.30
	Marjorie Skinner	A	·	·	·	·	·							12
	Phyllis Rowe	·	·	·	·	·	·	·	·	·	·			✓ 12.30
25	Margaret Mullins	·	·	·	·	·	·	·	·	·	·			✓ 2
	Dorothea Griffith	·	·	·	·	·	·	·	·	·	·			2.30
	Helen Martin	·	·	·	·	·	·	·	·	·	·			3
	Marie Greenwall	A	A	·	·	·	·	·	·	·	·		✓	3.30
	Violet Fleming	·	·	·	·	·	·	·	·	·				✓ 4.
														4.30
														5
														5.30
	Saturday													
	Geraldine Thomson	·	·	·	·	·	·	·	·	·	·	·		✓ 9.30
	Mildred Edwards	A	·	·	·	·	·	·	·	·	·	·		✓ 10
	Audrey Parton	·	·	·	·	·	·	·	·	·	·	A		✓ 10.30
	Olga Lewis	·	·	·	·	·	·	·	·	·	·			✓ 11
	Violet Fleming	·	·	·	·	·	·	·	·	·	·			✓ 11.30
	Rosemary Beckett	·	·	·	·	·	·	·	·	·	·			12
	Betty Staples	·	·	A	·	·	·	·	·	·				✓ 12.30

Plate VIII *A page from Victor Booth's attendance book while teaching at the Royal Academy of Music*

One of the main difficulties in learning pianoforte technique is to know how to let go partially and then pick up these 'holding' muscles.

The purpose of letting go a little or a lot of arm weight is to provide a basis against which the pressing muscles of the fingers, hand and forearm work to better advantage.

The two sensations of letting go and picking up can be cultivated by the following exercises (A, B and C).

A. This is for the arm only.

Place the fingers almost touching the lid of the piano, which brings the under side of the wrist over the white keys (Pl. II*c*). Now let the shoulder muscles go and the released weight of the arm will lie on the depressed keys (Pl III*a*). This weight is held there by slight pressure on the under side of the wrist. Next pick up the arm by contracting the shoulder muscles. For tenuto leave enough pressure behind on the under wrist to keep the keys depressed. This is purely to learn the two sensations of 'let go' and 'pick up'. There should be practically no visible movement in the tenuto form of the exercise.

This letting go and picking up of the shoulder muscles should now be played as a game of 'balance' and 'release', 'balance' and 'release' at the rate of about one action to a second. We continue this game until we can realise just how much weight we do let go and how much we pick up.

Through this exercise we should eventually become sensitive to the possibilities of controlled relaxation and contraction of the shoulder muscles.

B. The forearm is the bridge between the upper arm and the hand and fingers, so its sympathetic working with that member is essential. Before the following exercise can be practised it is necessary to have mastered the 'balance' and 'release' exercise discussed above, so that a certain measure of control of weight has been established. Now lay your hand on a table or your knee. It naturally lies on the outside (or little finger side of the hand). This then is the natural or relaxed position. Now on the keyboard put the hand into playing position. The work of the forearm muscles is now absolutely apparent,

D

without them, in fact, it is impossible to hold the 'playing' position at all.

If you 'rock' the forearm towards the thumb (a slight contraction) and allow the hand to fall towards the little finger (a slight relaxation), it will soon be appreciated that the forearm plays a great part in distributing the weight of the upper arm wherever it is required. For example, a slight contraction towards the thumb will help to sing out inner melodies in contrapuntal writing. A relaxation or leaning towards the outer fingers allows top melodies to 'sing out' above the lower voices. The flexibility of the lower arm is a great ally of ours in good piano playing.

It is surprising how many quite advanced players make so little use of these most helpful movements. In the early stages exercises for the forearm are found at the beginning of all good primers. I would hesitate before buying one without these preliminaries. For more advanced players the following exercise may be found helpful:

Assume the balanced position of the upper arm and place the hand over any five notes (either black or white) on the keyboard. Roll the forearm towards the thumb then towards the five finger. Gradually assume release position depressing the keys this time to the sound. Then reverse the process. This measures the weight required to produce certain dynamics when asked for in any piece being worked at.

To proceed:

In balanced position now go to the sound, and as weight is released from the shoulder position a crescendo results. Now reverse the process and a softer tone will be obtained. These movements can be timed to the metronome, increasing the speed as facility is gained.

The lateral roll is reduced when the thumb alternates with finger 2, and increases as the other fingers further from the thumb are employed.

The terms piano and forte here are relative pp–mf is just as possible as piano forte. In fact all degrees of tone are made easier with these adjustments of weight.

If preliminary practice is necessary a table top can be used. Make use of natural movements as much as possible. A good pianist makes playing look a simple matter, which it certainly is not. However, using the heavier and lighter parts of the arm for the tasks for which they are most suited is a step in the right direction.

C. The third exercise has a similar purpose, but it brings in the fingers.

Choose a table or any hard surface. Enough pressure coming through to the finger-tips will automatically induce relaxation in the big muscles in front of the shoulder.

Cessation of finger pressure will cause an immediate response of contraction in the shoulder muscle.

Immediately finger pressure ceases this big muscle resumes the work of holding up the arm.

When the fingers contract the shoulder relaxes, and vice versa, when the fingers relax the shoulder contracts.

Gentle pressure at the finger-end will mean slight relaxation at the shoulder.

More pressure needs more relaxation. Effort and cessation of effort should always be a balanced combination. They should increase or decrease in immediate response to each tonal need.

(2) The general condition of the hand should be hollow, making an arched position from finger to wrist. The knuckles should be at the summit of the curve (Pl. III*b*). Against these all finger pressure must react upwards. This hollow hand position can best be learned by placing the fingers and hand round the kneecap, making a kind of cup (Pl. III*b*). This arched appearance must be retained when the hand is lifted on to the keyboard (Pl. III*c*).

(3) The most important movements in piano playing are, of course, those of the fingers. These movements must be as free and unrestricted as possible.

As in walking and running all leg movements are easy and unexaggerated, so in playing the piano the fingers should move freely and without exaggerated movement. The first stages of these movements, those towards the key, can be learned on a table or on the tops of the keys.

Preliminary Finger Exercises

(Pl. IV*a*) Keep the thumb down and lift the four fingers, then allow each one to drop singly, in the order, 2, 3, 4, 5. In the final position all five will be down (Pl. IV*b*).

(Pl. IV*c*) In the same way, with the fifth finger down, raise the other fingers and thumb and then drop them singly in the reverse order, 4, 3, 2, 1. Again finishing all down (Pl. IV*b*).

Later on learn to lift and drop single fingers with the others all down—but this is much more difficult to do freely.

Although finger movements with the key going down and the preceding movements towards the key will ultimately merge into one movement, they are best learned as separate acts to begin with.

Movement with the key must be induced by pressure (exertion), whereas the preceding 'drop' movement towards the key is one induced by relaxation. The muscles used in the 'lifting' process have to learn to give way.

Broadly speaking, we have to learn to combine two definite and quite different tone-making sensations.

All so-called touches are bound to be a mixing of both of these.

One is the result of exertion and the other of relaxation.

But we must distinguish between two types of exertion: one which is positional and continuous, and the other which is tone making and momentary.

We are using the former whenever the fingers, hands and arms are held in position ready to play. So long as we keep this same position this exertion continues.

To become conscious of it is not easy. The reason is that we are engaged on what might be called a 'customary' action. We get so accustomed to sitting at the piano in a playing position, it is difficult to realise that this involves the making of any exertion at all.

Let us call this Sensation No. 1 (continuous).

Having made ourselves fully conscious of this, we now have to learn what it feels like to let go or relax these holding or positional muscles.

In the process of playing, this feeling of letting go is shortlived. So we will call this Sensation No. 2 (momentary).

It is really a loosening up to of the muscles before the tone-making effort is made. This last is Sensation No. 3 (momentary). It feels like a short-lived pressure at the finger-tip.

In reality it is a compound of exertion (of the finger, hand and partial forearm) and relaxation (of the partial upper arm).

As soon as we hear the sound we return to Sensation No. 1, but with this difference. If we are playing tenuto or legato we must use enough effort to keep the key depressed.

So we call this compound of two types of exertion Sensation No. 4 (continuous).

In this we learn to be conscious of 'holding' at the finger-tip and of 'holding' at the shoulder.

For Sensation No. 5 we must learn to feel exactly when we release the holding finger muscles and return to No. 1 positional sensation.

This all sounds very complicated. But it is necessary that we teachers should understand the process of 'playing' the piano from the point of view of combined sensations.

If the foresaid analysis is completely understood, it will be possible to deal with all touch faults on a common-sense basis.

It would be a mistake to attempt to go into these details with undeveloped pupils.

What we can do is to frame a series of exercises which will combine these sensations and develop technical capacity. Some of these can be done away from the keyboard.

One of the first to teach is hand movement from the wrist.

Clapping Exercises

The analogy of clapping the hands will explain the process.

Hold one hand still, palm upwards, and clap with the other one. A gentle fall of the hand into the other palm won't produce any clapping sound. Accelerate the fall a little and we begin to get the clapping sound. The greater acceleration of the falling hand, the louder the clap (Pl. V*a* and V*b*).

The 'control' of this fall is what we have to teach. It can either be held back or accelerated to a considerable extent. The acceleration should be gradual.

The extent of the movement should ultimately be reduced

to a minimum. The entire arm should feel that it works in sympathy with the hand.

Finally, do this exercise on the finger-tip of each finger in turn (Pl. V*c* and V*d*).

The finger being used adopts a nearly straightforward position.

One of the most generally useful exercises, and one that should be taught after the preliminary stages have been passed, is what we call

Pivoting Exercise

Every note we play becomes a pivot or jumping-off ground for every succeeding note played. Therefore every finger must be trained as a pivot for every other finger (Pl. VI*a*–VI*b*).

Pivoting can be done either from the top or the bottom of the key, but our first exercise should be with the key depressed.

The pivot must be held in place on the bottom of the key with sufficient pressure to give it security. Too much pressure will make for stiffness. Too little will mean that the key will rise. Comfort is essential but keyboard security must be maintained.

The movement to making the sound is chiefly made by a twist of the forearm away from the pivot. The finger and hand move slightly up into position to begin with, and then down for the tone-making impulse.

The touch is, of course, a combined one. It embraces all the essential actions used in tone making.

All the joints become involved in the sensations of reaction.

Pivot on 1st and play on 2nd finger.
Pivot on 3rd and play on 4th finger.
Pivot on 4th and play on 5th finger.
This exercise should then be done the reverse way, downward. Hold the G with the 3rd finger and play F, F, E, E, and D with

the 2nd. All adjacent fingers should perform these exercises daily.

The possible extensions between the fingers will vary with each hand's capacity.

Don't go to any intervals beyond one that is comfortable.

Obviously we can make further exercises if the fingers engaged become 1, 3, or 2, 4, or 1, 4, or 2, 5, etc.

All these exercises must be done in the left hand by reversing the fingering.

Further Finger Exercise

A simple formula for finger drill by numbers is: (1) Lift (exertion up); (2) Drop (relaxation); (3) Press (exertion down); (4) Release (relaxation) (Pl. VIIa, VIIb, and VIIc).

Finally combine all of these into one continuous movement. Begin with the finger resting on the key surface and finish with it in the same place from which it began.

Hand Touch Exercise

This same formula can be used in teaching hand touch. The movements made are only of the hand from the wrist. The exercises are best practised on one finger at a time held slightly forward.

It is important to study this formula closely, so that obvious muscular faults of stiffness or slackness can be dealt with on a common-sense basis.

One of the first essentials in daily practice is to establish muscular consciousness of the weight of the keys and hammers.

Our muscles must be educated—through our awareness of the opposition these offer when we try to move them at different speeds.

Exercises for Judging Key Movement

(1) Place the five finger-tips on top of any five adjacent keys. Gently move these down and up without making any sound.

This movement of the keys should be made by a slight movement of the whole arm.

The weight of the keys and hammers—moving so slowly as not to cause sound—can easily be realised and judged by this simple exercise.

(2) Increase the hammer movements, so as to make soft sounds, is the next step.

Gradually increase the hammer movements by more energetic movements of the keys until the sounds are louder and louder.

(3) Now successively swing a less and less number of keys; first (a) four, (b) three, (c) two and finally (d) one key only.

The less the number of keys moved the less the weight involved and the more difficult it is for the muscles to feel the opposition offered.

Exercise for Arm Swing on Finger-tip

Let us now proceed to what is the first important daily exercise in laying a foundation for technique.

Its purpose is to teach the arm to release weight momentarily on to the point of each finger in turn.

This is the way to set about it:

Put the pupil in a comfortable position for playing; the arm balanced, the hand hollow, the wrist loose, the fingers lying on the key surfaces. Test for freedom in the forearm by moving the wrist up and down, then in the upper arm by moving the elbow in and out.

The pupil now depresses some key with the middle finger and holds it down gently throughout the exercise.

The wrist should be gently moved up and down and at the same time the elbow moved out and in.

The movement of both wrist and elbow should be only an inch or two in extent and always gentle and on the slow side. Actually it should be at the rate of about one swing to every second.

Pressure in the finger-tip is now gradually added each time the wrist swings down and the elbow swings in. This pressure is the tone-making impulse and should be practised from the gentlest effort to the strongest.

It is only momentary and ceases the instant the wrist begins to rise and the elbow begins to swing out.

Every time the finger presses, the big muscle which holds up the arm relaxes. The amount of relaxation should balance the amount of exertion in the finger-tip.

Learn to do this exercise on each of the other fingers in turn.

This tone-making impulse learned thus as a sensation with the key held down must now be used for the purpose of actually making a sound.

This can only be accomplished by key movement. So we must learn to apply it from the top of the key to the sound.

Pressure 'to' the sound at the finger-end should always come in response to an imagined tone.

In making this there must always be perfect teamwork between fingers, hand, forearm and upper arm. Let all co-operate is the advice to give.

Gently throw everything into the finger-tip and make it feel that the pressure there controls the force of the swing of the hammer. The amount of force used will be dictated by the amount of tone required.

Imagine more and more that you are joined to the instrument. In other words, you are an extension of it. This is easier for violinists and cellists when contact with the instrument in a physical sense is much more complete as all these instruments are extension of the human voice, imitated by metal, wood or a combination of both. This physical contact is an important factor.

Exercise for Developing Correct Arm Condition

In rapid passages, when our combined touch works successfully, we should feel that most of the work is being done by the fingers.

Actually, although they make the principle movements, they should never be called upon to make undue exertions.

If the condition of the arm behind the fingers is right, then their operations will be free and successful.

If the arm condition is wrong, no amount of time spent in practising is likely to yield any satisfactory results.

There may be various ways of reaching this ideal condition, but one sure way is to concentrate on hand movements from the wrist.

In making these, if the wrist is too firm we quickly tire. If too slack, the results are negative.

There is a proper distribution of tension and relaxation which has to be found.

And the upper and forearm must be allowed to work in sympathy with these hand movements.

Here is the exercise, which should be included with those we do daily:

Hold the hand level with the forearm an inch or two above the keys.

Drop it to the sound. The key will be carried down by hand weight only.

Repeat these actions several times.

Do this without arm co-operation or pressure of any kind.

Now do this exercise by numbers. Count one, two, slowly. Lift and hold the hand at one, drop it at two.

Keep on repeating this movement, and, while doing it, gradually implicate the whole arm sympathetically. The correct feeling is that the arm subsides with the hand.

Although we begin this exercise with up-and-down hand movements about one to the second, these should be gradually increased to about four to the second.

As the hand movements become quicker they are less obvious. Ultimately they are merely felt as vibrations in the arm.

If the passage is not too fast there may be a conscious arm vibration for every note. As the pace increases this is not possible.

Then the conscious co-operation of the arm may be for only every alternate or third or fourth note. The metrical accentuation of the passage will determine where this takes place.

In every case the free movements of the fingers predominate and they should feel that they do the majority of the work.

No doubt hand pressure, as well as hand fall, is incorporated into this combined touch used in rapid passages.

It has been necessary to go into rather long detailed explanations in regard to these exercises because of their great influence in developing technique.

Obviously the last exercise cannot be used until the pupil is reasonably developed. All the others should be undertaken as soon as possible.

Exercises for Movements Towards the Key

A certain amount of daily practice should be done on the tops of the keys. Any technical study or portion of a piece can be used for this purpose, and the movements should be made 'in time', at a reasonable pace.

These movements are induced by relaxation. The fingers and hands fall without pressure on to the tops of the keys. These must show no movements whatever. If they do, it is a sign that some pressure has been used.

When the pupil is sufficiently developed, some of these exercises can be dropped. Some, however, must continue to be used for a short time daily until the sensations and actions for which they stand have become a second nature.

In order in which they should be used, these are:

(1) Arm swing on the point of each finger (a) from bottom of key, (b) from top of key.
(2) Judging key movement.
(3) Movement towards the keys
(4) Pivoting.
(5) Developing correct arm condition, avoiding stiffness in the upper and forearm.

Having educated our muscular attention with these exercises, we can now undertake methods of practice with some hope of success.

5
Musical Sense: Expression and Style

*Units must be taught before phrases and phrases before
sentences.*

When giving a lesson on a piece of music which has been in
our teaching repertoire for many years, which of us has not had
a sudden moment of revelation? 'Yes, this is how this piece
should be played. This is what the composer intended.'

These moments, alas, are rare, but they do occur from time
to time, but not unless the correct approach to making musical
sense of the studied piece has been the object of basic analysis
by both teacher and taught. When this has been undertaken,
and only then, will inspiration visit us.

At this point, this quotation from Robert Louis Stevenson
seems appropriate, 'The motive and end of every art is the
making of a web or pattern'. From this definition we recognise
the need to unravel the musical web.

Music as a language relies for its sense upon the recognition
of small and large sound groups. The ability to find these is all
important. It is a major difficulty that always faces us with whatever music we wish to teach. And here, perhaps, in our thinking
of music as a language, Herbert Spencer's definition, 'Music is
the idealisation of the natural language of the emotions', helps
us to understand what we are about to undertake. All higher
knowledge is gained by comparison and rests on comparison.

The western art of music in particular being that of the only
civilisation to have developed a harmonic system (Prof. D.
Tovey), its language has been artificially built up by a combination of Pitch and Time groups. These are arranged and
developed possibly with some inspiration, and certainly in the
case of so-called classical music according to some preconceived
plan. Thus if music is to be intelligently rendered the groups
which form the plan must first be discovered and recognised
as entities—in addition they must be compared one with another.

The 'expression' of music relies primarily upon these comparisons which are made between the varying tensions of Pitch and Time. As the pupil develops, expression may become to a certain extent intuitive, but we are never completely free from the obligation of deliberate comparisons. Naturally in the case of advanced students, these comparisons will take a slightly different form such as more detailed analysis of chord, progressions, etc. However, no comparison is possible without first of all group recognition. The importance of this point cannot be overstressed.

It is in reality the only basis upon which we can hope to build musical thought—in a small or big way.

Musical sense means logical musical thinking and we must discover some method of explanation to develop this capacity. What we wish to do is to lay a good foundation for musical understanding and so to open the door to 'reasoned' expression.

One of the main objects of this book is to point the way to right beginnings, so let us discuss this in the simplest possible way. In order to do so we will rely on the accepted principle of proceeding from the 'known to the unknown'. This demands the finding of some workable analogy. Let us take the one between speech (known) and music (unknown). There are many obvious similarities between these two mediums. The 'unit', the 'phrase' and 'sentence' are to music what the 'word', the 'phrase' and the 'sentence' are to our everyday speech. Thus we perceive that the musical 'unit' like the 'word' is a complete entity.

In both speech and music it takes two or more phrases to make a sentence. The advantage of using this simple analogy is that it can be used at every stage of musical development.

These facts can be easily proved when speech and music are listened to with concentration and intelligence, as without these last two attributes no real listening is possible.

But now we come to the difference, and a very considerable one, which exists when speech and music are written. Without some previous expert training it is often very difficult to 'find' the units on any written page of music, because so little help is given to the eye by our musical notation.*

* It is ironical that musical ornaments—such a stumbling block to many pianists—are the clearest for the eye to read, as they are the oldest signs in musical notation giving true indication of rising and falling pitch.

If speech were written in the way that music is written it would be as if someone was giving us a page of syllables and telling us 'This is a poem'. Before we could possibly read it, we must first put the syllables together to form words. We should then have to group and punctuate these to find the length of the lines, and possibly compare the rhymes.

Finally, we should recognise the metre. Then—and not until then—we should be in a position to get even the 'sense' of it. But it would require a good deal more thought and insight before any expressive reading of this syllabic poem could be given. Punctuation groups written speech into phrases, and this is all we have or need. The sense of the punctuated group of words will ultimately determine the expression and give us the climactic points.

In reading written music the reverse is the case. Frequently the 'expression' has been carefully indicated but the sense of the music is by no means obvious—the bar lines and grouped quavers, etc., seldom, if ever, punctuate the music. Their most obvious use is only a metric one and points the way to simple accentuation. Thus melody and harmony have to be considered before the beginning and ends of the longer 'rhythmic' shapes can be established. This important difference between reading written speech and written music should be carefully noted. It probably explains why students often put the cart before the horse and try to be expressive before being sensible.

As our ultimate aim is to stimulate 'imaginative' qualities, this pulling of the musical cart to pieces puts a considerable strain upon our ingenuity, our efforts to make this side of our teaching musically attractive. Very naturally pupils are eager to get to the piano. They want to play and hear the music. This attitude deserves every encouragement, but at the same time we must be careful to instil musical thinking. Unless the groups are clear in the mind of the pupil, the fingers cannot be called upon to make musical sense. Here it might be helpful to study in the lesson time a short section of the piece on which we are engaged; preferably separate hands point out fingering—groupings of notes, etc. (these points are dealt with in detail later in this book), until the student learns to approach all music with respect and caution. These habits can be learned, and it is never too early to start them.

Finally, they save time and, as students are usually intelligent beings, and have over a period of time learned to trust the teacher's judgement, it should not be too difficult to instil this basic training. In other words 'Make the fingers the servants of the mind'—students will soon come to recognise that this sort of work leads to really intimate knowledge of the musical text. Finally, 'Intimate knowledge becomes the foster mother of feeling'.

Seeing and *listening* to music are the two senses we both need to develop in our students well beyond the ordinary every-day pitch of observation. How to develop these in the musically uneducated mind demands a very definite plan of action:

(1) Establish a feeling for key-centre and tonality. (By singing the scale in tonic sol-fa from doh to doh.)

(2) Explain the general plan.

(3) Compare the identity the rhythmic groups by similarities and differences in the time patterns. Draw attention to masculine and feminine endings. The latter has one or more sounds (played gently) after the accent.

(4) Explain the terms 'weak' and 'strong' in regard to beats and bars and place the accents accordingly.

(5) Name and compare the intervals. (To sing them helps.) And note the pitch direction. This is a further aid to the identity of units. Draw attention to any modulations and accidentals.

To transpose the melody is a good aid to identification of a movable key-centre.

This method of simple melodic analysis draws attention to what is fundamental to the apprehension of the underlying sense in every melody.

General as well as musical education might always begin with some explanation of well-known tunes played as in accompanied melodies. The singing of the triads and chords introducing the harmonies may well come later, after the features of the melodic line have been established.

Let us now discuss—how we should proceed. Only two examples are given, and they have been deliberately chosen from the opposite poles of any pupil's development. This has been done to show that the same method of analysis applies in each case.

To use a universally known tune, let us take as our first example 'God Save the Queen', known as 'America' in the United States where it is sung to the words 'My country, 'tis of thee'. We begin by playing the scale of G slowly, thus establishing that tonality. As stated above, get the pupil to sing it, preferably unaccompanied, particularly noting the semi-tone interval between the 3rd and 4th and 7th and 8th degrees. A small explanation can be added as to the great difference between a tone and a semi-tone, and what these two intervals add in feeling to a tune.

Nothing could be simpler or more direct than this melody. The economy of means is extraordinary. The range is small—only a minor 7th. In my estimation this is no sudden inspiration, but as we shall see, the work of a highly trained composer who thoroughly understands the relative value of pitch and rhythm.

Thus is fulfilled requirement No. 1 in our plan of action. *Under No. 2* we point out that the complete melody consists of 14 bars divided into two main sections of six and eight bars. The first section begins and ends on the key-centre or tonic, and the second begins on the 5th dominant and also ends on the tonic. The beginning of the second section on the dominant links this tune to a probable folk song origin, since many of the oldest tunes in the world contain a literal repetition of Tune 1 a fifth higher either tonally or rhythmically. This, however, has been avoided tonally here as one might expect from a sophisticated musician.

These explanations which on paper seem so long winded, could be gradually introduced over several lessons. This type of work is to make one's student think musically and is only

intended to show the teacher that the many aspects of a so-
called simple melody can be made a subject of much interesting discussion and is the beginning of true appreciation
which in turn leads to more progressive playing. *Under No. 3*
the rhythmical patterns of these help to establish their identity,
as can be readily seen from the diagram.

The rhythmic and partial pitch sequences are much clearer.
All the units have feminine endings, except 3 and 7 which are
masculine.

The dotted rhythm gives remarkable unity to the whole.
Under No. 4, in section 1, the rhythmic movement is from
the weak bars (1, 3, 5) to the strong (2, 4, 6). These latter take
the main accents. In all the units, excepting 2 and 7, there is a
secondary accent on the 3rd beat owing to the sub-division of
the 2nd beat, but this can be omitted. Section 2 is built on a
similar plan to section 1, except for the extra unit, and the
quaver sub-divisions in the last two units. *Under No. 5* we discuss
the intervals and pitch direction. The whole melody is made up
of falling or rising 2nds with the exception of one 3rd in the first
unit, one 5th connecting the 1st and 2nd sections, and two 3rds
in the 6th and 7th units.

The highest note occurs in the penultimate bar of the last
unit. This is sometimes called the emotional climax. Lastly
we must again play the complete melody but in different keys—
say F or A, drawing attention to the new key-centre. (This last
exercise could possibly be of practical use to students studying
for the Musicianship Examinations held by the Associated
Board.)

Our second example is taken from Beethoven's 'Sonata

E

Pathétique', Adagio Cantabile, and one supposes that the
student at this level of attainment has, at any rate, an elementary knowledge of harmony, and of the main types of cadence,
which we find Grove describes as 'The devices which in music
answer the purpose of stops in language'. They are commonly
divided into three types. The Perfect, Imperfect, and the Interrupted. Nowadays we include a fourth, the Plagal (or Oblique).
Certain successions of chords do produce the effect of finality
(Plagal and perfect) suspense (the imperfect) and, in the case
of the interrupted cadence, we hear the music being literally
interrupted, as if being sent in a new direction. The progressions
in the bass determine these effects, and they must be generally
recognised by the student, before analysis such as the following
can be undertaken.

Adagio Cantabile

Printing the units as above, will make the similarities and
differences in rhythm, pitch and recognition of cadence points
much more obvious. After establishing the key of A♭ Major,
go on to mention and explain the two accidentals: E♮ as a
passing note whereas A♮ implies a change of key. This bar 8
melody divides into two phrases, each of four bars. The first
section consisting of two, 2-bar units both having masculine
endings on the dominant, whereas the 2nd section has two 1-bar
units plus a 2-bar unit with feminine endings on the tonic. Point
out that similarities of ryhthmic pattern occur in the 2nd section

only. There is an increase of sub-divisions of the beat preceding the cadences in the 2nd and 5th units.

The rhythmic swing is from the weak bars 1, 3, 5 and 7 to the strong bars 2, 4, 6 and 8—where the accents fall.

The intervals and pitch direction need a good deal of explanation in this very beautiful tune. In the 1st section the first notes of bars 1 and 2 are identical. In the 1st unit we have a falling 2nd and a rising 4th to the accent. In the 2nd unit, however, we get a falling 5th to the accent (in an inversion of the previous 4). So one has an octave range.

In the 2nd section this falling 5th is the prominant feature and is used by Beethoven in a most masterly way. The first notes of bars 5, 6 and 7 and the following five quavers make a falling scale series The range is only a 7th when playing through the complete melody, with the accompanying harmonies it can be pointed out that sensitivity to changes of key such as occur in bar 6 is a help in building up musical sense, which finally gives the key to expressive playing. Few of us fail to be moved by the beauty of the descending diminished five in bar 6, which follows so unexpectedly after the similar drop of a perfect five in in bar 5.

However, musical sense must be put first always, so we have now put the horse in front of our musical cart instead of the other way round.

We see that in this chapter we have endeavoured to educate our students in some of the ways in which musical language becomes intelligible. It is no longer a series of sounds, but as at a certain time a foreign language suddenly becomes comprehensible (after a good deal of study), musical language becomes our mother tongue.

Patience is a great virtue, and is needed always, and by our own example we must show that 'she has her perfect work' in teaching musical language. Patience is no negative virtue. Patience works and waits but with a vision kindled by enthusiasm. When we reflect that the last word stems from the Greek entheos (possessed—by the gods) our lesson times should perhaps help us to experience that moment of revelation mentioned at the beginning of this chapter. 'This is how it should be played—this is what the composer intended.'

There is no doubt in dealing with musical expression that we are all in general agreement with the aforementioned quotation by Herbert Spencer that 'music is idealisation of the natural language of the emotion'. Plato goes into greater detail:

Music gives a soul to the Universe

Wings to the mind

Flight to the imagination

A charm to sadness

Gaiety and life to everything

It is the essence of order and leads to what is good, just and beautiful

Of which it is the invisible, but nevertheless, dazzling, passionate and eternal form

This makes, indeed, great claims for our art of music, but it certainly guides us into realising the power that music has over us and its ability to heighten and underline dramatic moments; vide, the background music in drama and, above all, in opera where music carries on where words can no longer express the emotion of love, hate, fear or anger. Whose mind has not taken wing on hearing the theme (Andante, molto cantabile ed espressivo) of Beethoven's Op. 109, and what sadness we feel is not lightened when we have listened to the second movement of Mozart's Piano Concerto in C minor (K457)! Music does play upon the human soul in an extraordinary manner.

As music has this power (and we all acknowledge even if we do not understand it) how important it is to choose the right piece at the right time for our students. It can 'give flight to the imagination', or do the very opposite. It can lead to all 'that is good, just and beautiful' or perhaps destroy the delicate musical growth already accomplished by former study. However, when the right piece has been chosen and been made musically sensible we must probe much more deeply into what might be called the technique of expression. This implies very careful and concentrated listening; in other words, to develop the piano ear.

The student who has full marks for aural tests in musical examination does not necessarily have this special equipment which must take careful heed of the tonal possibilities and limitations of the piano. To listen to oneself is very difficult. It is part of knowing oneself and as Burns said: 'O wad some Pow'r the giftie gie us To see oursels as others see us'. Substitute 'hear' for 'see' and we will readily appreciate the task ahead of us. The arts lack a special language with which we teachers can communicate our ideas one to another. We are, therefore, forced to borrow and make do with an everyday vocabulary. This makes our task more difficult.

Expression and communication in music rely very much upon 'phrasing' and this is the real test for the performer as it is intensely individual. This dividing of music into intelligent and sensible groupings can be allied to breathing. Both are a mystery. Breathing can be long and sustained or short as we will, according to the dictates of the phrase to be sung or spoken, but it is controlled by the sense of the words. So, singing a phrase in one breath can throw light upon it, but the harmonic claims have also to be considered and in truly musical people this equalising of the tension between harmony and melody is often intuitive. For those not so fortunately endowed we have to be more explicit.

I once read in an article on 'Musical Performance' in an important daily newspaper: 'The ultimate test of musical performance and its mystery is phrasing. That which gives distinctive character to an artist's interpretation of familiar music is his phrasing of it', and later on the article also states: 'and what the artist perceives are perpetually varying and minute differences of tonal force and speed'.

Personally, I am grateful to the writer of that article for stating the case for individuality in performance so clearly, but how do we train pupils to recognise these minute differences of tonal force and speed that the writer talks about? I think 'these differences' were probably intended as *his* definition.

There is an element of vagueness in both this and Grove's explanation of phrasing which is 'the proper rendering of the phrases . . . in an intelligent and attractive form'. So we must endeavour to be more explicit. I have added the following explanation. 'Phrasing in music is a comprehensive term, it includes many expressive details and is used to indicate the manner of communicating musical thoughts. Individual performers present the rhythmical groups, giving sense and personal expression through the sensitive use of legato and staccato and of the above-mentioned use of tonal force and speed.'

Having then stated the essentials for phrasing, we will now suggest how to begin the education of the pianist's ear in the light of them. In this type of training concentration plays a great part. No true listening is possible without this second element.

We can work under several main headings, but let us deal with *tone* first :

The student must realise that single sounds can have both tone length and tone quantity. So let us keep the first exercises simple and deal with the length only.

Exercise 1   (a)   Play any note as softly as possible and hold the key down. The pupil should indicate the exact moment the sound can no longer be heard.

           (b)   This exercise can be repeated with a louder sound when of course the fading out will take longer. This is a very important lesson—to learn the limitation of tones instrument, i.e. the piano as an instrument of diminuendo. There is, however, one very important exception to this fact which should be demonstrated as soon as possible.

           (c)   Make a sound as before but rather loudly. Hold the key down and about a second later depress the damper pedal and hold it for two seconds (still holding down the key). Then let the pedal up for two seconds. Repeat this up and down pedal movement until the sound dies away. A 'bulge' in the tone will be noticed at each pedal depression, owing to the added vibration of the related strings. A marked decrease in tone will be noticed when pedal is up.

               Many beautiful effects can be obtained with this pedal technique which will stimulate the pupil to experiment for himself in pieces which have long sustained notes. It is no wonder that Chopin called the pedal 'The soul of the piano'. 'It causes the sound to breathe.'

(d) Ask your student to listen carefully to the difference between a damper pedalled sound and an unpedalled sound. Then similarly with the left (or soft pedal). Finally, listen to a sound with both pedals depressed.

(e) The following exercise gives a more exact measurement of the duration of sounds. Whilst the student beats a steady 4 up a bar, play on the 1st beat a sound which can be of varying duration. Anything from a semibreve to a semiquaver serves. The student by careful attention can measure the exact length of each sound before its final fading.

Later on recognition of dotted notes can be added and of the four grades of staccato, staccatissimo, mezzo staccato and portamento. If a small part of the lesson can be given up to this cultivation of a 'piano' ear, pupils will progress rapidly.

Exercise 2.

These deal with tone quantity. Let us deal with six different tone levels, fortissimo, forte, mezzo forte, mezzo piano, piano, pianisisimo, cutting out the two extremes of loudness and softness.

(a) Contrast ff. with pp., p. with f. and finally mp. with mf. When the student can hear the differences, especially between the final pair, they will be on the road to real musical listening.

How many concert pianists could benefit from this exercise!

(b) Later on the difference between pp. and p., p. and mp., mf. and f., f. and ff. could be be added for further practice.

Lack of recognition of different tonal levels is a great hindrance to the student's progress in any sort of expressive playing and careful work and preparation is needed in this field.

How many times do we hear a soft passage played to us at a roaring forte! So it behoves us all to pay great attention to this side of our work.

Exercise 3

In this third set of exercises we are dealing with two or more sounds, so that tone graduation is added to those of length and quantity. Let us begin with two notes of different pitch in a rising scale series of falling 2nds:

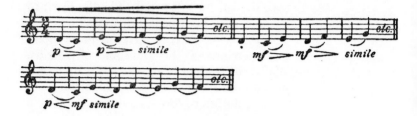

In the case of smaller units such as these, the increase of tone (crescendo) will be towards the accent and decrease (diminuendo) away from the accent. At this stage it would be a mistake to point out that the third type of phrasing often carries a decrescendo to the normal accent giving it a syncopated effect. Always proceed from the known to the unknown. Phrased in the three ways indicated, we must explain that the changed position of the bar line is responsible for the difference in the placing of the accents in the 1st and 2nd units. There are many other ways of phrasing this example. Here are two:

The pupil must learn to recognise the following details in regard to these examples:

(a)   Which sounds are louder or softer?
(b)   Which are the longer or shorter?
(c)   How are they grouped by legato and staccato? (In other words, how are they phrased?)
(d)   How many notes are grouped and inflected by each gradation?

This last exercise can begin to bridge the gap, and remove inhibitions which often prevent real personal identification by the performer with the music performed.

Suggestions for different tonal colourings can be given by hearing them played on strings or woodwind instruments, etc., and at varying pitches. Great stimulus is given by occasional sharing of a lesson with an instrumentalist other than a pianist. If this is not a practical suggestion, the whole set of exercises can be taped with varying instrumentation. This type of work can be very stimulating.

The proper tonal treatment of feminine endings calls for special notice. The amount of tone we give to the weaker note when it is due to be heard, should match the amount in the waning tone of the accented note.

This matching of tones is a pianistic device of considerable difficulty requiring a sensitive ear as well as a sensitive touch. Exercise 4.

We can make a fourth set of exercises for this effect. Here is one:

These foregoing exercises should be tape recorded and the 'play back' will soon reveal our weaknesses. Only perseverance will accustom the student to recognise tonal effects of length, quantity, gradation and the matching of sounds.

Once the phrasing of the single melodic line is concluded, we can turn our attention to 'balance of tone between the parts'. Exercise 5.

Play any melody and accompaniment (a Chopin nocturne or mazurka are unfailing examples which spring to the mind) and ask the student which part should predominate.

Scales in 3rds can be used in educating and stimulating this type of listening. The simple expedient of playing 1st bass and then treble louder can start off the process and technical ability for this type of work. Double octave scales can then be added, thus giving four parts which demonstrate the great differences possible. When one part predominates over the other three. There is probably no effect in piano playing which needs more skilful teaching than this one, and none which has a greater influence upon the artist and presentation of the music. The training of the muscles for the making of these effects often takes a long time and requires patience and perseverance.

Studies of course should be given to highlight all technical problems and work on the Chopin Études, both Op. 10 and 25, even if done with no view to public performance will yield much to teacher and student. They are a monument to all that is finest and ideal in piano playing and different artists' recordings of these masterpieces can be listened to with close attention. No technical problem is ignored or passed over.

Op. 10, No. 3 can be used for a further exercise in chord playing. Take for example the final chord in bar one. Play one note louder than the other, then reverse the effect. Progress then to chords of three and four parts stressing each note in turn from the lowest to the highest or vice versa. The use of this Étude for chordal exercises has the dual purpose of acquainting the student with some of the greatest musical literature for the piano, so he cannot but improve his technique at the same time.

Having discussed some problems of tonal expression we must now endeavour to give some help for the rhythmic angle. Tonal expression, of course, largely depends on the separation of the units, one from the other, and rhythmical expression has most to do with combining them. In this way is created a general sense of continuity of movement for the whole length of the phrase. Broadly speaking, tonal and rhythmical elements are the tension which give life to the music. Without a balance between the two, no real interpretation of the composer's wishes is possible. We have all heard of tempo rubato. Some of us have read much about what it is and how to teach it. Literally, of course, it means 'robbed time', i.e. a slight hurrying at the beginning of the phrase is to be repaid (exactly) by a slowing down in the latter half of the same phrase—or alternately one whole phrase accelerates to be repaid by the next phrase slowing down.*

The question of climactic points is always involved and whether the hastening is towards the emotional climax of the phrase (usually its highest note providing it falls on metrical accent) or its rhythmic climax (the end of the phrase or cadence point), the paying back of the robbed time must be exact. Usually tonal gradation contributes much to the effect with

---

* If a piece can be played in strict time, then with tempo rubato, we can gauge by a stop watch how exact has been our playing back of that 'robbed time'. This is a far better method than leaving it to instinct or intuition, always unreliable except in those most musically endowed. A.F.

a crescendo to the climax and a subsequent diminuendo. These points must be carefully considered.

Underlining, a type of shortened rubato, is another effect which can be successfully used. It is a slight lengthening of a note or chord which has the accent. This should always be slight and never enough to hinder the rhythmic flow of the phrase—or the regular pulsation.

Some pianists make use of 'delayed emphasis' but this should always be applied sparingly. The slight hesitation before an accent can be irritating if overdone. Taste must regulate its use, and the inexperienced player should in general avoid it.

Mood in Music

There is a remarkable essay by Herbert Spencer called 'The Origin and Function of Music' (published in Everyman series with the Essay on Education). To quote:

> 'The various inflections and rate of movement of the voice, which accompany feelings of various kinds and intensities are the germs out of which music is developed. It is to be demonstrated that these inflections and cadences are not accidental or arbitrary but they are determined by certain general principles of vital action and their expressiveness depends on this.'

In other words the mood or sentiment of any speech can be understood expressively spoken without understanding the language merely from:

(1) The rise and fall of the voice (pitch).
(2) The quantity and variations in tone (volume).
(3) The general rate and variation in speed (rhythm).
(4) The manner of speaking (mood).

It is not difficult then to gain the impression from the spoken word that terror, horror, tranquillity, grief, joy, human dignity, etc., is being expressed by the speaker (facial expression plays its part). (Instrumental teachers could benefit from the study of methods of training such as that given to opera singers or actors.) After all, sounds and movements heard and seen in everyday life (below and above the normally expected), produce some sympathetic response and thus we begin to see the ultimate connection between effects in speech and music.

All that makes for expression in speech, is used similarly in music.

The really thoughtful teacher sees that the student has the working knowledge of the classical forms such as Suite, Sonata and Fugue which is necessary for sensible and intelligent playing. Biographies of the composers studied should also be available for student use. Thus it will follow that the sounds of nature found so often in works of Beethoven and Schubert, for example, we owe to the fact that these two men often found their inspiration in the woods, and beside the streams of their native land. Mozart, on the other hand, as far as we know, never seemed to admire the landscapes through which he passed. However, to help in the interpretation of his piano music a knowledge of his operas (however superficial) can help materially in interpretation. Debussy, Ravel and the Impressionistic composers were deeply influenced by the writers and painters who were their contemporaries. A knowledge of the poems of the former can often give us the key to the right mood of certain of their pieces, and a loving study of the painting of the latter in the art galleries will also add inspiration and understanding. A tall order! But it must be faithfully carried out if the composer's intentions are to be conveyed as truthfully as possible, and this must surely be the aim of we piano teachers.

6
Methods of Practice

Practice is the name given to the essential repetitive work which we do to form necessary habits of mind and muscle.

It is the means by which conscious or voluntary acts ultimately become sub-conscious or involuntary, the process whereby we are enabled to do things muscularly at the keyboard more or less without thinking, leaving our thoughts free for the interpretation of the music. We are told that practice makes perfect. We might add, provided the practice is based on reason. It is very necessary to bring home to our students that one wrong repetition can do intense harm, whereas a correct repetition adds much on the credit side.

There is no vacuum or standing still in practice. It is forward or backward. This is a point which cannot be sufficiently stressed. It is easier to have trained any student from the outset of his or her musical career, than to take over another who already has many bad technical and musical habits.

It is the latter student who poses the real difficulty. The changing from bad to good habits is a double problem. We have to find a means to get rid of the old habits before we can ever begin to attempt to establish the new one. This requires much patience on the part of both teacher and pupil.

When a new piece is to be learned, it is essential that the right habits should be formed as soon as possible, and the chief among these is correct fingering. This must be learnt with its note as one unit. So perhaps a short digression here is appropriate before other methods of practice are suggested.

If fingering is neglected in the early stages of learning anything, it is very doubtful whether the Music in question will ever give satisfaction either to pupil, or teacher.

Fingering is of no use to us in performance until it becomes subconscious and the changing of bad fingering habits to good is a double and difficult problem. To save time, then, it is essential that the right habits should be formed as early as possible.

So let us begin our campaign for better and more correct practice.

(a) Repeat only the right thing.

Doing only the right thing, and the same thing over and over again is necessary, otherwise no habit, or worse still, the wrong one will be formed.

(b) Practise slowly in order to be able really to listen and be fully conscious of what we are doing every moment of our practice time; listen.

(c) Never too much at a time.

If to begin with we attempt to do too much at each repetition, we cannot recollect precisely just what has been done. The stage of the pupil's mental development must govern the precise amount given to be studied. The important point about these practice repetitions is that they must be frequent. What we appear to learn on one day would probably have to be repeated on several successive days before the correct habit becomes fixed.

We must remember three things in regard to every pupil.

(1) The amount of time available for practising.

(2) Individual aptitude for learning.

(3) The stage of each pupil's development.

These three considerations will naturally influence all our instructions, and also determine in each case our method of explanation. As practising is done when the pupil is alone, we must make certain that any suggested method of how to set about it is based on reason, and the type of reasoning which will appeal to the particular student's mentality. In addition, we must see that it is done at every lesson, until we are sure our advice will be carried out. As teachers, our object should be to train our students to do without us. Their ability to tackle problems intelligently without our help is the measure of our success.

Much so-called practice is a waste of time. This is proved by the poor results achieved and the long time it takes for some pupils to learn anything, even badly.

Very often these poor results are the outcome of tackling too difficult works—or practising too large sections at a time.

Proceed from the simple to the complex should be our motto!

The method used (repeating once over again a large section of the music) is an impossible one. The amount repeated may vary from sentence to half a page, or even a whole movement. Unless it is pointed out to them, how are these unfortunates to realise they have taken on an almost impossible task? A comparison with methods of learning prose or poetry helps to drive this lesson home (common sense should tell us that to attempt to memorise too much at a time, rather than starting with a few lines, is not the way to tackle the problem). A small section of the music should be studied first, and this usually helps in an understanding of what follows later, especially in the works of the classical composers.

All learning is memorising in some form or other. Piano pupils learn through at least three methods:

The mental (which embraces memorising of the harmonic progressions), the visual (imagining the page of music is still in front of you), and the muscular (finger memory).

The crux of the practice problem is how much can be visualised and remembered in detail—ideally no more should be dealt with at a time than can be retained in the memory. This does, of course, depend on the ability of the pupil. However, the simple does lead to the complex, and great results will be forthcoming if these procedures are carried out. The amount will naturally vary, but in all cases there will be a reasonable limit which must not be exceeded.

How to give a pupil appreciation of shape, mood and character belongs to the musical or expressive side of our teaching. How to produce the sensitive effects to these, forms the technical side.

We are apt to forget that learning to play the piano is a complicated process. Three senses are always involved:

(1)   The eyes read.
(2)   The muscles feel.
(3)   The ears listen.

Teachers must take careful note of these facts. If the individual education of any of one sense is neglected, then the pupil's progress is bound to suffer.

When reading music our mind works in two directions: vertically and horizontally. The former enables us to combine parts and realise individual harmonies; the latter to isolate each part and realise individual melodies.

In orchestral and vocal music, each part is written on a separate stave. In piano music, however many parts there may be, all are crowded in on two staves only. This makes piano music much easier to read harmonically, but the melodic lines may become confused and often difficult to isolate. Because of this, piano students may find contrapuntal music difficult to comprehend and also to play.

Teaching pupils how to look at music intelligently is one of our essential tasks.

How to develop the visual sense is a major issue for every musician, and the peak of this development has been reached only when seeing becomes hearing.

When we are able to read music in the same way that we read prose or poetry, we have reached one of the highest levels in musical education. This end should always be held within the pupil's view, but any detailed discussion of how to achieve it lies outside the scope of this book. All we can hope to do is to point the way.

The signs and symbols are obviously our stock-in-trade, and we begin with these. Notes should be regarded as degrees of some scale having a fundamental tonic or key-note. Their musical significance only begins when considered in relation to each other as intervals. The interval is the simplest form of group, and its recognition marks the first step towards regarding music intelligently.

Melodies and harmonies are all built up by intervals, so one might say very truly that they constitute the real musical alphabet.

There are three ways of 'practising' the recognition of intervals:

(1) Naming the interval made by the notes on the stave (the eyes).

(2) Finding these as keyboard places (the fingers).

(3) Naming the interval made by the sound (the ears).

The importance of using intervals when training each of the three senses involved cannot be overstated.

In drawing, before attempting to make a sketch of anything, the mental picture of the object must first be made clear. Similarly, before attempting to play anything it is equally important that the musical picture (made up of notes and details of tone and tune) should also be made clear. If we are not absolutely explicit as regards every detail we wish to teach, the pupil will be working in the dark.

When practising, make it clear to the student that the 'thought' should always be positive and definite both before and after each repetition; development will largely depend upon just how painstaking are the repetitions of both the thought and the act. Just as a child learning to walk develops his muscles at the same time as the habit of balanced movement, so does the piano student form fresh muscular habits for the hands and fingers when learning notes and finger groups.

A useful method of helping this 'positive thought' before and after each repetition, particularly in passage work, is to play:

(a) Slowly and heavily
(b) Staccato
(c) In varying rhythmic schemes with a 'stop' on the 1st or last notes of each group (give examples)
(d) 'Building' practice. Take a short passage and build: one note, two notes (stop), three notes (stop), etc., until the whole passage has had a stop on each note.

This is a great aid to real thought and concentration, for most mistakes in performance stem from our not knowing our pieces sufficiently well. By this means, and no doubt teachers will have their own suggestions to add, hesitations, stumbles and stops will gradually cease. New habits will be fixed and the subconscious stage will have been reached.

The notes and time now move along steadily, under involuntary control, and we are able to give our attention to expressing the 'nature' of the music without interruption.

How to introduce to a pupil any new music which is to be practised requires careful consideration so that the musical side comes first and is never lost to sight. Unless the pupil is sufficiently developed to begin work independently, some such procedure as this should precede any advice on practising:

(1) Play the piece through, then talk about its tempo, mood and character.
(2) Play it through a second time and find out by questioning how the pupil responds to the 'nature' of the Music.
(3) Explain the general plan of the piece, and the formal details. First take its main sections, then its phrases, and finally its units. In this way the pupil's appreciation of shape will be awakened.

Reasoned analysis may not be possible but related melodic

F

features can easily be pointed out and discussed, and a pupil can soon be taught to appreciate the different cadential effects.

(4)   Finally play the piece through a third time, when the pupil can listen with a new interest and follow the shape and plan of the music as well as realise its general character.

Some of this advice has already been given in the previous chapter, but I feel it also rightly belongs here, and therefore must be repeated.

One must never tire of reminding pupils that to try and overcome several difficulties at the same time is a mistake. This only causes delay and mental frustration.

Once we have established the general conception of any piece, discussed its shape and pointed out the major difficulties to be overcome, we should advise the pupil how to proceed somewhat in this manner:

(1)   Learn the notes and the fingering.

(2)   Attend to the length of the sounds. These will either be held (tenuto), connected (legato) or detached (staccato).

(3)   Learn to play small sections of from two to four bars (approximately one phrase length) at a regular steady pace and slightly stress the normal accents.

To elaborate:

(1)   When the student is learning notes and fingering we must bear in mind natural limitations and the need for thinking in groups. Care should be taken that no more notes and fingers are involved at each repetition than can easily be remembered.

If this advice is followed literally, it will surprise many how readily the fingers will fall into correct positions and how quickly the student will form correct habits. These must be recognised singly before being combined.

(2)   With reference to the length of sounds.

In tenuto, in addition to attending to the length of any single sound, we must see to it that the finger holds the key down freely, with enough pressure to give it security.

The test for freedom is to move the wrist up and down and the elbow out and in, so slightly that it is hardly noticeable.

In legato (which is really connecting several 'held' notes), we must be very careful to train the giving way of the sense of security (or pressure) on one finger, and transferring it to the next—in other words, we must learn to 'walk' on the tips of our fingers, where the pressure is slight but continuous. Good legato is probably the most difficult thing to teach in piano playing. The ear of course plays an important part. Careful listening for the smooth passing of one sound to the next, so that the chain of sound is unbroken, will do much towards acquiring it. It is better to practise it softly at first, so as to avoid too much pressure in the making of the sounds.

Successful teaching of staccato also demands careful training in listening, as we have only to make sounds, not to hold them. The sense of finger security is very slight, and can be felt only on top of the key before and after the sound. It sometimes helps to explain to your student that in legato, the finger rests at the bottom of the key and, in staccato, on the top.

(Some teachers prefer to teach staccato first).

According to most text-books, there are several grades of staccato, and perhaps the technique of teaching it would be simplified if they were referred to as different grades of tenuto. After all, any sound longer than the very shortest requires to be held for a fraction of time.

(3) When learning to play to a regular pulse, pupils must first be taught to indicate the beats giving the pace, and while beating time, to think the music. This is one of the ways we shall eventually link up the look of music and the rhythmical sounding of it. It should always be persisted in and good results be bound to follow.

With reference to accents. The accented beat in music may be compared to the accented syllable in words. We must remember we learned words much earlier in our development than music, so that musical accent is more difficult for us to apprehend. It is unlikely that anyone would mispronounce such everyday words as today, tomorrow, yesterday. If, however, these are expressed in rhythmical units of music such as:

these are not in everyday musical usage. We can never be certain that any implied accents will be correctly placed unless we repeatedly point them out—listen for them, and insist on the careful tonal treatment of the weaker notes— naturally the notes not marked with an accent must be played gently.

Our first examples are taken from Schumann's Album for the Young (Op. 68). This is a unique set of remarkable teaching pieces.

The difficulties range from Numbers 1 to 6 (which can be given to Grade 1 students) to Number 40 (suitable for Grades 7 or 8). Most of the pieces differ considerably in character and each presents tonal and rhythmical problems of considerable musical importance.

The moods cover many emotional phases from grave to gay.

It is a pity that all the pieces are written either in duple or quadruple time, but variety is gained by several being in compound duple. Most of these are of a lively disposition and most attractive musically.

Numbers 1, 3 and 5 are alike in character and difficulty, but for rhythmical reasons we chose Number 5 as the most suitable to begin with. Throughout this piece the bar lines are placed before the accents, whereas in Numbers 1 and 3, these come in the middle of each bar (excepting for the three main cadences in Number 3).

As bar lines generally indicate accents on the beats immediately following them, it is better not to start right away with an exceptional use of them.

It is important to point out that a bar in music consists of an accent, a prefix and a suffix. The sum total of these makes up the full value of the bar, but the prefix can begin anywhere, on any beat, or portion of a beat.

All three pieces are in common time and in the key of C. We awaken musical interest by playing through No. 5 to the best of our ability and pointing out that the nature of the piece is quiet and unobtrusive that this mood remains throughout; that it has a soothing quality, is song like in character and consists of a melody and an accompaniment.

The composer gives only two indications, which establish the mood: one Nicht schnell (not fast) which suggests the speed, and the other 'p' (piano) the tone level. Before playing it through a second time we briefly explain the plan of the piece. (These preliminaries do not take long to discuss.)

It has two 8-bar sentences (the second of which is repeated), both of which are divided into two 4-bar phrases which further sub-divide into four 2-bar units. All the units end at the half bars and the cadences are alternately masculine and feminine.

After playing through a second time, we draw attention to (1) the similarities and differences in pitch and rhythm (the formula A, B, A, C, and D, E, A, C, indicates these); (2) the modulation (at the end of the second unit) and (3) to the accidental C ♯ in the left hand. (Unit A, 2nd sentence.)

Formula Of Units: A+B+A+C : D+E+A+C: .

We begin our practice by taking each hand separately in units.

The first right-hand position is completely normal and covers the first unit. It is indicated by putting the second finger on E. The fifth falls on the top A and the thumb on D. There are no gaps between the fingers. This can be proved by holding all five fingers down (D, E, F, G, A).

The pupil now beats time (or claps) and indicates a slowish pace before playing the unit. A sufficient number of repetitions are now necessary until it moves along without undue hesitation.

If the legato is unsatisfactory, that must be attended to next.

We must be satisfied with a reasonable result to begin with. Perfection will only come by degrees.

The left-hand first unit has two hand positions to deal with. It begins with the natural five-finger position (no gaps, fifth on C, thumb on G) for the first eight quavers. At the beginning of the next eight quavers, the hand must open outwards to enable the fifth finger to reach the B. Once this movement is made (and remembered), the other fingers follow each other naturally (no gaps). The next step is for the pupil to indicate the pace and 'think' the two quavers to each beat.

Now come the practice repetitions, preceded by preliminary work on top of the keys to show exactly where and how the hand changes its position.

The teacher having indicated how to set about learning the notes and fingering in the first unit, the pupil will be in a position to follow the same method when learning the rest of the piece.

The hands should now be put together unit by unit. At first only the notes and fingers can be considered.

As these gradually go together, an attempt can be made at a moderate speed to play to a regular pulse.

The pupil must be content to learn every detail unit by unit. (1) The tone levels in each hand; (2) the gradation of tone; and (3) the balancing of the two tone levels when the hands are put together are each separate difficulties.

Finally, when the piece is ready to be played at the correct Tempo, the Music should first be imagined or thought while the pace is indicated.

Number 8, 'The Wild Rider', is our next example.

This is a totally different type of piece to Number 5. It is in 6/8 time and in the key of A minor. As the title suggests, its character requires a lively movement. The Tempo indication is, in fact, 'lively' (Lebhaft). It is played staccato throughout except for the two main accents in each phrase, which are tenuto and marked sf. The general tone indication is only mf. Here, as is usual, the crescendo is towards the accent, and the diminuendo away from it, but no gradation is marked by Schumann.

An important point to be remembered when playing pieces in compound time should be noted here: the first note of every triplet takes a slight accent regardless of the rest of the context. This means that the second and third notes of the triplet will be played softer by comparison with the accent, thus establishing the duple beat.

The general plan of the piece consists of three sentences of eight bars each (A, B, A). The middle sentence has the melody in the bass and the key changes to F major. This and the first sentence are the only two shown in our example.

Each phrase of four bars sub-divides into one 2-bar unit, and two 1-bar units. The cadences are all feminine endings. The tonal gradations follow the pitch, which rises to the second bar, and falls to the fourth in every phrase.

The notes of the first unit are nearly all part of the chord (A, C, E) of A minor. There are three finger groups in the right hand, which must be dealt with first. The fingering of the second

WILD RIDER

unit is identical with the last bar of the first unit, although the notes are different, and the third unit keeps the same hand position as the second.

As in the last example, fix the notes and fingering of each unit separately before combining them. In the left hand, the only difference in the hand position is made by the thumb, which has to move.

More tone must be given to melody notes, wherever these lie.

The accompanying chords must in each case be with less tone. The gradation of tone is chiefly felt in relative accentual values. Each of these tonal aspects must be cultivated separately before being attempted in combination.

The phrasing in bars 2 and 3 requires careful practising.

As the pupil advances, every piece presents fresh difficulties. They may have to do with:

(1)   The rhythm.
(2)   The tone balance (see Chap. 4).
(3)   The holding of certain notes while others are detached.
(4)   The acquisition of speed.

Teachers must contrive to invent preliminary exercises of their own, dealing with each difficulty separately.

The reason for each exercise should be explained to the pupil. In this way much time will be saved, and the practice repetitions of the whole piece can be cut down considerably.

Here are a few examples taken from Schumann's Op. 68, which will explain how to set about this aspect of our work.

Example 1 (For rhythm). The placing of the F ♯ is the difficulty.

From No. 9

In all cases similar to A and C, it will be found that pupils invariably play the F ♯ too soon. The mind is, of course, not thinking correctly. If a sound is made (as in B and D) in place of the rest (in A) or the dot in (C), and several practice repetitions are made first with the sound and then without it, this difficulty should soon be overcome.

Example 2 (For speed). The difficulty here is to get the notes to move along fast enough.

From No. 11

The first principle to grasp in dealing with this, is that one short group (from the first of one beat to the first of the next) is much easier to control and develop than two or more groups. The two single groups (marked B), if persisted in, will soon prove this point.

C and D are further examples of how to alter the value, in order to get small groups that will move quickly. The quavers give time to think each note, but the semi-quaver group must become a single thought.

We get an analogy for this type of thinking with words. With long words such as 'exaggeration' which contains five syllables, each syllable can be thought of separately. But such a word used in conversation slips into place as a single mental entity with no individual thought for each syllable. So what we have to learn is group thinking for speed.

The speed of all quick passages written in semi-quavers can be developed by this preliminary mixing of quavers and semi-quavers, the changing the one over for the other before attempting the passage as it is written.

Example 3 (For accents). The original (marked A) needs not only speed which can be dealt with as in Example 2, but also requires strong beat accents.

From No. 12

The best rhythm to adopt is that indicated at B. By waiting on the accented note this method gives an opportunity to listen and feel the rhythmical and tonal effects made.

The difficulty is to bring to bear extra force on the notes that are dotted and not on the semi-quavers which precede them.

The technical advice must be: 'Don't allow any help to participate *behind the fingers* that play the semiquavers. Save this up for the dotted notes that follow, then the hand and even partial arm can be added'.

Example 4 (For harmony). Schumann writes the whole of this study in an unbroken 6/8 quaver movement.

From No. 14

The strong and weak bars, indicating rhythmic movement, are very difficult to find in this type of piece, unless the broken chords are first played together in 'skeleton' harmony. This has been indicated at B and C. In this way the shape becomes quite clear and the phrases can be moulded, both rhythmically (with slight give and take) and tonally (with gradations).

Example 5 (For alternating double notes).

From No. 29

The difficulty here is the alternation of double and single note semiquavers. This type of tremolo or shake occurs very often in more advanced piano music.

The best way to practise it is indicated at B. Pivoting first from the single note and then in reverse from the double notes.

Obviously more tone is required on the double notes, so for these some muscular help from behind the fingers is necessary.

Example 6 (For tone balance and rhythm).

From No. 26

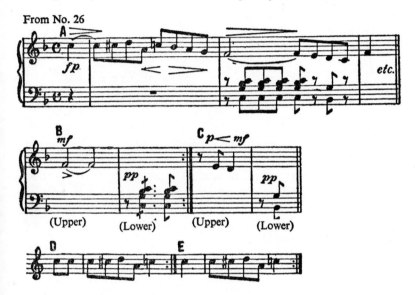

There are two difficulties to be overcome here. The first is a rhythmical one. It is to give sufficient length to the initial crotchet C tied to the quaver C in the first bar, so that the C ♯ comes in at the exact moment it is due. There is, of course, the added tonal difficulty of making the tone of the C ♯ match the end of that of the C. Each difficulty requires separate attention.

D and E are the preliminary exercises which ought to cure any rhythmical lapse. After doing these often enough, one must imagine the repeated C while this is held as in the original form A.

The second difficulty is tonal. Sufficient tone must be given to the minim F while the chords are played pp. In B and C the soft notes in the under parts must be practised separately before combining them with the melody in the upper part. The technical advice is: swing the keys more gently for the softer sounds.

Example 7 The difficulty here is to retain the legato in the lower part of the left hand while the thumb repeats notes in the upper part.

From No. 38

B and C indicate the preliminary exercises.

By repeating the crotchet Gs while the minim underneath is held, the sense of security on this minim will be cultivated. It is only another step then to connect B and C into one exercise so that the legato is made between the two minims. It may be necessary to play the Gs staccato to begin with, but later they should be as tenuto as possible and the thumb should never lose contact with the key.

7
The Damper Pedal

The success of every appliance depends upon the intelligence
with which it is used.

The damper pedal is a most important aid to the expressive possibilities of the piano. It enriches the quality of the tone and exercises a great influence over the character and phrasing of any music that is performed.

Its two main potentials are to sustain and to intensify. All sounds heard with the pedal down are bound to be affected in both these ways. But to decide just 'what' and 'for how long' we should sustain or intensify is often a big problem.

A famous pianist once said: 'The art of the foot is as great as the art of the fingers'.

When to let the pedal up is perhaps more important than when to put it down, but both these considerations continually arise.

In the case of the experienced player the ability to produce pedal effects has become second nature. The right foot moves up and down in immediate and unconsidered response to the musical intention. But a long period of trial and error with conscious effort has to elapse before anyone can use the pedal in a subconscious way.

In the early days, what we must cultivate is an attentive and critical ear for possible pedal effects. But before this the following mechanical facts must be demonstrated and proved to the pupil.

(1) When the pedal goes down, the dampers go up. So long as the pedal remains down, sound will continue (in diminuendo of course) for the obvious reason that the dampers are held away from the strings.

(2) When the pedal comes up the dampers go down and settle on the strings. In this way sound is stopped or damped, as the name itself suggests.

The pedal goes down. The pedal comes up. These two movements must be practised separately. They sum up the why and wherefore of all pedal technique.

How? When? And for how long?, as applied to both these facts, are the teacher's pedal problems.

The first (How?) can be answered by considering the best method of moving the pedal.

(1)   With regard to the going down:

The action of the pedal lever on different pianos varies very considerably.

Sometimes the lever gets loose and the response of the damper movement is not immediate. The exact moment when the dampers begin to rise cannot be physically felt, because the muscles employed are insensitive and untrained to this kind of judgement.

The only real medium of control is the ear. And this is where our pedal education begins and ends.

If we listen carefully we can detect exactly 'where' in the down pedal movement the dampers do leave the strings. It's a mistake, as a rule, to push the pedal down much beyond this point.

The less movement made by the foot (either up or down), the better for sensitive results. It becomes purely a matter of judging how far the dampers must be held away from the strings to allow sound to continue.

At the very first lesson in the use of the pedal this should be demonstrated.

Another important point is that the sole of the right foot must rest on the pedal and never lose contact with it, and the heel should remain on the floor. The sole should certainly not be permitted to be held an inch or two above the pedal.

Always try to cultivate what has been called 'invisible' pedalling. This means keep in touch with it and use as little down-and-up movement of the pedal as possible consistent with intended effects.

(2)   With regard to the coming up of the pedal:

The extent of this movement is, of course, governed by how far the pedal went down. If the dampers are held too far away from the strings by a complete pedal depression, and the movement of the rising pedal is sudden, the falling dampers are bound to 'bump' on the strings. The unmusical bumps thus made can often be heard even in a concert hall.

Many performances are spoiled by this clumsy type of pedalling. When it has become unconscious and habitual it is very difficult to eradicate, and is best avoided by implanting only right ideas to begin with.

It is important to remember that when we say 'Change the pedal with each change of harmony', the word 'change' includes both the up and the down pedal movements. Failure to appreciate this fact is probably responsible for much smudgy and unclean pedalling.

Ineffectual damping is caused by the dampers not having time to stop sound because the foot goes down too soon after it comes up. Or it may be, it did not come up far enough to allow the dampers even to reach the strings.

First exercises in pedalling should be framed in the light of the foregoing statements on 'how' the pedal should move to the best advantage without involving any sounds at all.

If these exercises are to include 'when' the pedal moves, the movements must be made 'in time'.

Exercise 1 (As an example)

(a) We count 1, 2, 3, 4, and keep on counting sharply and not too fast. The pupil is at first instructed always to put the pedal down on 1, and to let it up on either 2, 3 or 4 as the case may be.

Then (b) down on 2 and up on 3, 4, or 1;

or (c) down on 3 and up on 4, 1 or 2;

or (d) down on 4 and up on 1, 2 or 3.

These simple exercises in pedal movements by numbers without any sound must be taken seriously and undertaken during several successive lessons. If persisted with they will save much trouble later on.

The second problem, 'when' does the pedal go down, is a musical one. It involves a close study of all intended musical effects.

This also decides our third problem: 'for how long' should the pedal remain down or up?

Exercise 2. The first exercise in 'possible' pedal effects with sound would be to play without depressing the pedal any single low note such as the low D at (a).

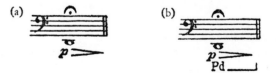

Hold it for some time and listen to the amount of sound.

Then play it again with the same force, but this time with the pedal down as at (b). Draw attention to the difference this makes in tone intensity. Keep on playing and holding this sound, and do this several times alternately with and without the pedal being down. In this way the difference in effect should become obvious to even an uncritical ear.

Now we must prove 'why' there is an intensification of the tone.

Exercise 3. This time hold the low D down without sounding it. Point out that the damper is held away from the string while the key is down. Now play loudly (at crotchet speed).

Depress the low D without sound and hold silently but sound the upper notes

These sounds will be partially communicated to the low D-string which will vibrate in sympathy because the notes of the chord of D are related to low D. Give this demonstration two or three times.

Exercise 4. Now again hold down the low D without sounding it, but this time play:

Depress the low D without sound and hold silently but sound the upper notes

If the piano is reasonably in tune there will be no responding vibrations in the low D-string. In other words, there will be no sound, because the chord of D (flat) is unrelated to the low D.

All that is now needed is an understanding of what is meant by harmonics or upper partials in relation to any sound, and since this can be acquired from any book on the Elements of Music, there is no need for an explanation here. It may possibly be beyond the grasp of young children, but at least we can demonstrate, as we have shown, that certain sounds are related and others are unrelated to each other.

It should next be demonstrated how the pedal sustains several sounds.

Exercise 5. With the pedal depressed, play a chord in arpeggio:

Hold it down until the sounds die away. This demonstration should be repeated several times both piano and forte.

At each repetition the pedal should come up at different points in the waning sound, as indicated in our example.

Listening to the sustaining power of the pedal is an essential exercise in educating the 'pedal' ear.

All examples of pedal effects with the pedal down should be preceded by listening to the same example played with the pedal up.

When the pupil understands how to control pedal movements and how to make these at given moments in time, and in addition how sounds can be intensified and sustained, then, but not until then, we can introduce the most usual effect of all, that of 'legato' pedalling.

Unfortunately, many teachers have little idea of teaching anything else about the pedal excepting this. All its other uses are taken for granted.

So our next exercise is the connection of sounds by means of the pedal.

G

Exercise 6. For this purpose we return to Exercise 1, but this time with the additional difficulty of making sounds.

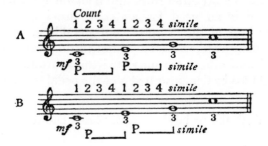

The pupil is instructed to count 1, 2, 3, 4 and to play the notes of the chord of C; but these must be played with the same finger, so that no finger legato is possible.

When the pedal goes down on 1 and up on 4, it will be observed there is no connecting of the sounds. When the pedal goes down on 2 and up on 1, the sounds are connected.

After our previous demonstrations of what happens when the pedal moves down and up, the pupil should be able to explain why the sounds are connected in the second instance and not in the first. It is essential that we persist with this exercise until this explanation is forthcoming and until some proficiency has been gained in connecting sounds in this way.

It would be as well to begin any discussion of 'when' to use the pedal with some general definition such as the following:

Definition:

The pedal may be depressed and changed with each change of harmony, provided this does not interfere with melodic clearness, the phrasing, or with details of duration.

Notice the word 'may'. There is an important difference between 'may' and 'must'.

Although there are occasional places where the pedal must be used, as a rule it is a matter of taste whether to use it or not.

One is frequently asked the question: 'At what stage of a pupil's development should the use of the pedal be taught?'

The answer to that question is: 'As early as possible, but as seldom as possible.'

For examples let us again take the Schumann pieces from Op. 68.

In Numbers 1, 2 and 3 no pedal is required; but in Number 4, 'Ein Choral', the use of the pedal is necessary. This piece must be played legato. To connect even small chords with finger legato is too difficult for pupils in the earlier grades, so we have to train the pupil to connect chords by means of the foot.

This does not mean that Number 4 should not be attempted without using the pedal.

On the contrary, it should be persisted with until some finger legato begins to develop. There could be no better exercise for this. But it is doubtful whether a really satisfactory result will be achieved for some considerable time without the help of the pedal.

In Number 5, the pedal could be used at the cadential points for phrasing.

The pedalling of legato chords and cadential points will give the elementary student quite enough to think about to begin with. The fingers and hands are so busy at this educational stage that it would be a mistake to attempt more than a minimum of pedalling.

In deciding 'when' to use the pedal, one must take into consideration several conditioning factors:

(1) Whether the sounds are above or below middle C (approximately). (The duration of a sound varies according to the length of the string. The low sounds have longer strings so these last longer than the high sounds. These in fact have so little duration that the shortest strings have no dampers at all.)

(2)   Whether the chief influence lies in the right or in the left hand.

(3)   Whether the influence is harmonic, melodic or has to do with duration and phrasing.

(4)   Whether, because of the type of music or for purposes of contrast in effect, it is better left alone.

It is necessary to discuss these conditioning factors in some detail.

The position and number of passing notes must influence all our decisions in regard to pedalling.

If these are much below middle C we either leave the pedal alone or it is changed for each passing note. If they occur above middle C there is much greater freedom possible. The reasons for this have already been given. But again we must notice whether the passing note is mixed up with a general harmonic effect, or whether it is one of a series of melody notes.

It is always a moot point with teachers just how many melody notes, if they are moving reasonably fast, should be included in one pedal depression. The best pedalling is always on the side of economy of use. But there is always the case of long arpeggio basses when the low bass note must be retained throughout, otherwise the fundamental note of the chord will disappear. In such instances the clearing of melody notes in the right hand must give way to the superior needs of sustaining the left hand.

As a matter of fact, what happens in the left hand is usually the predominating influence in most music which requires the use of the pedal.

In deciding 'when' to pedal, rests and staccato marks are always a puzzle for teachers. Are they intended and essential to the required effect or have they been merely put in because the composer was thinking in terms of 'touch'? That is the question.

Many composers, after Beethoven, have complicated our pedal decisions by writing in rests and staccato marks and at the same time put in pedal indications which nullify their written intentions in regard to duration.

There is much conflict of opinion on this subject, but usually careful thought and experiment will solve the problem.

All music by composers before Beethoven and especially that by Haydn and Mozart, can be interpreted precisely as written in regard to all duration marks. The less we use the pedal in such music the better.

The easier contrapuntal music is better learned without any pedal. As the pupil advances with this type, almost without exception, only short pedal depressions are possible, and here again these may be only effective at cadential places.

When playing contrapuntal music there is a method of pedalling often used by advanced pianists which gives a gentle buzz to the sounds. This effect is got by holding the dampers so close to the sounding strings that the vibrations are only parti- ally damped. Some teachers refer to this as half-damping.

Personally, I don't think it is an effect that can be used satisfactorily except by the expert.

There is another effect which some people refer to as half- pedalling. This is got by a rapid 'up-and-down-again' move- ment of the foot, which must be sufficiently fast, so that the dampers do damp the upper sounds but do not damp the lower ones completely. It is an effect which can always be used where, in the upper register, a series of chords is written over a low bass note, as in the well-known C ♯ Minor Prelude by Rach- maninoff. Certainly this effect should be taught whenever the music demands its use.

The trouble is that the sonority of bass notes in most school pianos is so poor that the effect cannot be properly demonstra- ted.

As I have stated earlier in this chapter, pupils frequently only learn what is called 'legato' pedalling, to the total exclusion of every other type.

There are of course many instances when the foot should go down with a chord or note and not afterwards. This is especially noticeable in extended chords which have to be 'spread'. In this case the pedal must catch the lowest bass note, or a false harmonic effect will result.

Or take the low bass notes in pieces such as a Chopin Waltz. It is dreadful to hear the attempts to play these with 'legato' pedalling. Either the low bass notes are lost and only the upper chords are caught, or the up-and-down footwork is so rapid that the harmonies are smudged. There is no satis- factory clearance.

In such cases the pedal must go down with beat 1 and come

up on either beat 2 or 3, whichever effect is the better. To keep the pedal down for the full bar is almost invariably wrong.

The following examples are taken from Schumann's Op. 15 to give some indication of how the teacher's mind should work, reasons are given for the pedalling chosen.

Example 1. Number 1.

We must consider the harmony, the melody and the duration. The harmonies change for every beat, so unless there is any melodic reason, or one to do with the rests, the pedal will change for every beat. But if we use legato pedalling for A we ignore the rests in the bass part and give the same effect as in B. Here Schumann has carefully written in the bass part with the crotchets, without any rests, therefore it is reasonable to suppose he intended the rests in A to be literally interpreted. Bearing in mind these statements, we now know what to do.

In A the pedal is depressed 'almost' with each beat and released on the third quaver of each triplet. If the pedal goes down a fraction late, the legato melody notes in the top part will have a chance of being cleared.

In B simple legato pedalling is used: the pedal being depressed after each beat and coming up with the following beat as indicated.

Example 2 Number 2.

In the first section of this piece we have to take note of rests and phrasing as well as of the harmony and melody.

The joining of the third beat to the first of each following bar is the most obvious effect, so we can decide on the pedalling for this right away, down on 3, up on 1 is the advice to give.

But we are still left with two more chords to deal with: the semi-quaver followed by the crotchet. The former is short and must be light in tone, so we decide not to pedal this chord. The crotchet chord could be connected to the third beat by a legato pedal (the lower indication). Personally, I am in favour of a shortening of this crotchet just a fraction, and so allowing the 1-bar unit to be slightly detached from the following one: therefore we decide on a short pedal effect.

The advice to give is: down on 3, up on 1; down on 2, up before 3; and this holds good all through the A section wherever the units are similar.

When we come to the B section there are no rests, and there is a doubled melody to deal with. All of this is well above middle C. So we have a certain amount of freedom allowed in regard to the passing notes.

Either of the two pedal markings could be adopted, but the keen ear will be in favour of the shorter pedals, as these give a clearer melodic line.

Example 3. Number 5.

In the A section of this piece the influence appears to be chiefly melodic. That is, the pedal effects will be legato with a change for every melody note.

There is only one harmony to each bar in this excerpt. If

harmony were to be the predominant influence, we would get the lower indicated pedalling, but the effect produced would blur all melody notes, and take no notice of what must be regarded as essential rests in the left hand. The influence, therefore, must be melodic.

In B we get a rising series of melody notes over a tied octave in the bass.

When melody notes rise in this way (especially if there are no passing notes en route) the effect of pedal blurring is nothing like so obvious as it would be if the melody notes were to fall.

So in this case we decide to sacrifice melodic clearness for the sake of the obviously intended 'tenuto' harmonic effect. Either the top or the bottom marking could be adopted.

When we consider what might be regarded as faults in pedalling, these can either be of commission or omission.

Of course the actual pedal 'technique' may be bad (discussed at some length earlier in this chapter).

But presuming this is reasonably satisfactory there are other faults which, if recognised, can be avoided. Therefore it is as well to keep a list at hand of these common faults in pedalling:

(1)   The first most obvious one occurs when the pedal is held down through several changing harmonies. It is incredible that even the dullest ear could put up with much of this mixing of harmonies. The fault will usually arise because the player's attention is fully engaged in finding the notes or playing them in time —at any rate the attention is not fixed, as it should be, on the sounds.

If we demonstrate both the right and the wrong way with some persistence and say, 'Listen to this', this type of bad pedalling should soon begin to shock the pupil.

(2)   The second, but much less obvious fault, causes a smudging of two harmonies. It occurs when the up-and-down movement of the pedal is either too quick, or the up movement is incomplete. In either case the dampers cannot fulfil their functions. This is perhaps the most common fault with all pianists.

The only cure is to think of the up-and-down movement as separate actions with a slight hesitation or pause between the two. This slight pause will allow the dampers to do their work properly and stop all trace of the previous harmony.

Again the player's aural attention must be directed to the sounds.

(3) The third fault is the smudging of melodic lines: keeping the pedal down through too many passing notes, especially when these occur below middle C. This fault becomes very apparent in contrapuntal music.

Where the finger legato is poor, or when the note values are not held, students at once fly to the foot in order to cover up these deficiencies.

The only cure for this is to leave the pedal alone until the legato and tenuto are improved. Then we point out where the short depressions may be used for this or that reason.

If it is a slow melody in the bass and the pedal can be used for each note without being clumsy, it becomes merely a case of changing it often enough to clear each melody note. The reason it must be used is to give sonority to the melody tones.

(4) This fault might be termed 'spoiling the phrasing'. We must include in this the ignoring of essential rests and staccato marks.

It is especially noticeable in the music of Haydn, Mozart and Beethoven, so much of which relies for its effect upon the phrasing details of legato, and staccato.

The common fault is for the student to try and use legato pedalling for the harmonies and completely disregard all the phrasing details which have been so laboriously indicated by the composer.

Here again, the fault probably arises, to begin with, through a lack of finger legato and tenuto, and possibly to inability to combine different types of touch in one hand.

We must demonstrate this fault very carefully and direct the pupil's aural attention to the correct interpretation of the details. In addition, we must show the muddled effect produced by using legato pedalling for each harmonic change. The only possible short pedal depressions must be clearly proved.

(5)   This fault arises from changing the pedal too frequently at probably the beats, and not keeping it down long enough for the sustained harmonic effect intended.

Very often in pieces which are analogous to a song with an accompaniment, the latter consists of long arpeggio figures which must be sustained by the pedal. Some occasional pedal changes may be necessary for melodic reasons, but to change the pedal for every melody note or every beat, as some students do, is disregarding the more important influence, which is harmonic. Again the best way to cure this fault is to demonstrate first the right and then the wrong effect.

(6)   Another common fault is failure to 'catch' low bass notes with the pedal. This fault is most noticeable in pieces where the left hand skips to notes or chords that cannot be connected by the fingers.

Genuine legato pedalling is not possible with this type of bass. If it is attempted the foot cannot get down before the hand skip has begun, and the bass note has been released before the pedal goes down.

The cure is to pedal with, not after, the low bass note.

When all is said and done, we are forced to the conclusion that good pedalling depends upon sound musical judgement and an educated ear.

The foregoing advice and exercises can only be regarded as elementary and pointing the way.

Once we have laid some kind of sensible foundation we can then only leave it to musical taste to do the rest.

8

Repertoire, Fingering, Sight-reading

Repertoire.

At the very outset of our teaching career we are faced with a difficulty which will pursue us throughout the whole of our music teaching lives. The question which is always insistent is 'What music am I to give to this pupil?'

It is quite obvious we must have a nucleus with which to begin operations, and this is the reason why, in examinations for any teacher's Diploma, some knowledge of repertoire is essential.

When we begin teaching, our first pupils are probably beginners. Do we know how to start them off? If we don't, the obvious course is to seek assistance from a book. There are many such helpful text-books. Two which spring instantly to mind are Mrs Curwen's *Teacher's Guide* (still one of the finest) and Joan Last's *The Young Pianist*. Both of these have the advantage of having Primers which carry out the suggestions in the actual text-book in a practical sense on the keyboard itself. See also bibliography.

Regarding very first books the following are well tried. *Making Music* (Blake & Capp), *Off we go* (Diller-Quaile), Mary Donnington's *The Way Ahead* and Christine Brown's *First Album*.

The list is long and most teachers like to find a book which suits their own particular ideas, but do not automatically turn to the most recently published—many of the newer tutors are still inferior to *First Steps in Musicianship* by Matthay-Craxton-Swinstead. Try to study as many as you can, for each makes some contribution. If they assist you to develop your own method (one of Mrs Curwen's great tenets) they have justified their existence.

A little further along the way, no teacher can afford to neglect the *Mikrokosmos* of Béla Bartók. These 153 pieces from the earliest stages (they pre-suppose a knowledge of lines and spaces) are a monument to its composer and, at Bartók's own suggestion, can be taught alongside the Anna Magdalena Bach Book and the Schumann pieces to which reference has already been made. No young musician could have a finer foundation on which to build.

A useful approach to 'the Moderns' is Hindemith's *Wir Bauen Eine Stadt,* and a little further on, when our repertoire book is being planned, reference will be made to further additions to more recent approaches.

With these publications any teacher has ample material not only for dealing with pupils in the beginning stage, but also for their much further development.

I make these concrete suggestions because each of the books I have mentioned has the cause of good music at heart and can assist in laying the right foundation from the very beginning. This is all-important, and anyone beginning to teach on the lines they recommend begins with a correct musical outlook and with a plan which is the outcome of years of experience.

Every teacher should start a 'Repertoire' book and plan it on the lines of some well-known examination system. It is a mistake to accept anyone else's repertoire without proving its value by our own teaching experience.

The Associated Board grading is from I–VIII and is, on the whole, well-planned, although it is a pity that more studies are not provided to prepare students for the modern trends which these days do come thick and fast. The exercises in the *Mikrokosmos,* Books 1–4 (usually found at the end), are excellent material but alas! there is not enough of it.

The repertoire book should have a few pages for each grade with three columns on each page headed Technical, Classical and Modern. As the pupil advances there will have to be more detailed classification. For example, under 'Technical' we have finger exercises as those of Schmitt, Hanon-Plaidy or Beringer. For the more advanced, Bauer, Philipp and the Brahms 51 are all sound.

The studies of Czerny, Burgmüller, Heller, Cramer and the invaluable Clementi can be added. The Books of Studies of the Associated Board are an excellent guide and the answer to the pupil's technical difficulties can usually be found therein.

However, for the independent, most publishers these days have reliable graded lists of studies so the choice is a wide one.

Under the heading 'Classical' we come upon so vast an amount of music that it is bewildering to know what to select and how to classify. In the easier grades we might distinguish between a few definite types of music such as: (a) The easier J. S. Bach and Handel pieces and similar period music.

These should lead to the study of Bach's Two and Three part Inventions which are among the foundations of keyboard playing, and should never be neglected. They lead directly to the Forty Eight Preludes and Fugues (see bibliography) to which they bear a direct relationship keywise. Compare the first of both the Two and Three Part Inventions with the corresponding C major Fugue Subject (Book 1).

Purcell, Clarke, Hook, and some of the older English composers are now appearing, well edited, and arranged for the piano. A good deal of research is going on into the work of eighteenth-century English musicians, and excellent teaching material it is proving to be.

   (b)   Sonatinas. These might be by Clementi, Kuhlau, Dussek, Beethoven, etc.

   (c)   Lyrical pieces such as the easier song-like pieces by Schumann, Mendelssohn, Schubert, Tchaikowsky, etc.

   (d)   Characteristic pieces such as the 'Wild Rider' and 'Knight Rupert', from Op. 68 of Schumann.

There are, in addition, excellent modern pieces by British composers such as Swinstead, Alan Richardson, Malcolm Williamson ('Travel Diaries' introduce many of the modern techniques in a simple form), Leslie Fly, Cyril Dalmaine. All of these have made excellent contributions and no teacher need be short of interesting and stimulating material. It is a practical suggestion to be on the mailing list of good publishers. In this way one is kept in touch with the newer trends, as well as better editions of well-known classics.

Among their foreign counterparts in Rumania and Hungary are splendid pieces, many of which are in various styles showing modern trends and introducing serial techniques.

The Russian Kabalevsky has probably made the greatest contributions, with his host of charming pieces, including many sets of easy variations, invaluable in teaching.

As a preparation for the music of Debussy, the French Collection of 'Jardin d'Enfants' and the 'Pièces Ingenues' of Jean Clergue, are delightful and will be found to appeal even to the most unimaginative pupil.

The important point is to build our repertoire with great care. Music should be studied carefully first by the teacher, and never turn down a suggestion from your student or pupil. We can learn valuable lessons from each and all of them. Never give pieces that are dull and too long no matter who the composer is. An attractive repertoire is the thing to aim for, and should also include well-tried favourites.

Viewed from the angle of the advanced performer, grading elementary music is difficult to do well. When choosing music for any particular grade, certain aspects of every piece must be taken into consideration. The following list will suggest the sort of questions that should arise in the teacher's mind before making any decision.

(a) What is the pace? How many notes are there to each beat? Are there many black notes to deal with? (The pace is always the regulating influence).

(b) Are many of these outside the five-finger position of the hand? Are there any scale or arpeggio passages? (Extensions and the passing of the thumb must be noted.)

(c) How many parts have to be combined? Are there any places where there are two or more parts in one hand?

(d) What are the time difficulties? Are the rhythmic details likely to cause trouble?

(e) Is the phrasing consistent between the parts? Are there any places where one part is held while another is detached?

(f) Is the necessary pedalling difficult?

(g) Are there any octaves, trills, turns of extensions over the octave?

This list by no means gives all the possible questions that might arise, but at least it includes those which are more immediate.

Pupils with small hands have a habit of wanting to learn pieces with octaves and big chords. It is much better to discourage this and endeavour to get them interested in pieces that require neat phrasing, and some agility.

It is well to remember that the size of the repertoire does not regulate its value, but the building of it can become of very genuine interest if one begins with the right fundamental outlook.

A good plan is to make notes in the repertoire book: the name of the pupil, and the date when used, will help to stimulate the memory. We should note the mood, whether bright, tranquil, vigorous, a mixture of several moods, or whether the piece is fast or slow. Whether it requires finger dexterity or has to do with chords—all such aspects should be noted.

As we advance in our teaching, it is essential to broaden our outlook and get to know an ever-increasing number of works by composers of note. We must always be open to new ideas and acquaint ourselves with new trends, even if they are not acceptable and we do not agree with them. The mind of a good teacher is never closed to the music of the future. After all, as Vicent d'Indy so wisely remarked, 'music will go whither the next composer of genius directs it'.

Sight-reading

Pupils must hear sounds before they can imagine them. Attract the pupil's attention to certain facts—first simply and then in combination.

When a boy of fifteen, I entered for an advanced musical examination and got very good marks for everything, except for sight-reading. This side of my work had been completely neglected and consequently was little better than what might be termed 'spelling'.

Shortly after this experience the pianist of our local Choral Society fell ill and I was called upon to fill the gap. I remember the first work to be studied was Handel's 'Messiah'. Our 'orchestra' consisted of the piano, one violin and one occasional flute. The piano was therefore expected always to be in the foreground to give the leads and to hammer out the melodic lines. The singers were nearly all very raw material and most of them without previous musical experience.

In those days, I suppose, I possessed the sublime confidence of ignorance; at all events I had the impertinence to imagine I could fill the post, and I proceeded to rehearsal and attempted to sight-read 'Messiah'. The results should have been humilia-ting, as I had been much too lazy to put in any practice, but the confidence of youth prevailed and I got through somehow.

What the general effect of those early rehearsals must have been I will leave to the imagination. Our conductor was a cultured amateur, one of the patient long-suffering variety, who, I presume, did not like to admonish in case he lost his pianist.

He instructed me to watch him, follow his beat, and to play something in the way of notes so as to keep things going. But that 'something' of mine must have been much more of wrong than right notes. While the singing went on, I suppose these did not matter so very much, provided that I kept the time going.

As the rehearsals proceeded, I, of course, became more proficient, and I was able to see and find the right notes more quickly.

By the end of the second year, we had laboured through three more choral works, and I began to take some pride in really trying to read accurately. I think I am justified in saying that by that time I had become a tolerably good sight-reader.

I relate this personal experience in detail to show that, whatever the circumstances may be, the hard road of practical experience is the only road to follow.

To become a good sight-reader one must have confidence and plenty of practice. Pupils should be made to do some sight-reading at every lesson.

To aid the teacher there are some excellent graded methods introducing one new point at a time with varying rhythms to clap and become familiar before the actual pitch is introduced. Mrs Curwen's Sight Reading books are excellent, and in more modern times, Joan Last and Markham Lee, among others, have both produced excellent material.

But as with learning anything, there is always a right and a wrong method of approach to it. Mine to sight-reading was certainly a very clumsy one. With proper guidance I could have saved much time. But where I was particularly fortunate was being told that 'keeping time' was more important than accuracy of notes.

Reading at sight has obviously to do with 'the way we see' music. Pianists not only have to use this visual process, but in addition, the notes read must be instantly translated into keyboard places. The finding of these, demands an almost automatic 'muscular' response before the act of playing can take place.

And when we say 'the way' we see music we mean the immediate mental application of whatever musical knowledge we happen to possess, the subconscious use of all we have absorbed about the language of music, which enables us to translate and sense and expression of what we see. This ability to give expression to the small and large sound groups as they unfold themselves while the eyes travel forward, naturally depends upon training and development.

It is a mistake to give the pupil sight-reading material that is too difficult as this merely discourages, so we need to have plenty of material for every grade. It can be used in two stages. First as pure reading at sight, second in discussion as to what went wrong, and a replay correcting the mistakes.

This is a help to quick study which is really a branch of reading. The student then is less likely to make the same mistakes again, once this analysis has taken place.

This then is our ultimate aim and object—the reading of rhythm, melody and harmony at one and the same time. But of course, before this happy combination is possible, each must be developed separately, and by the method mentioned above.

Help along these lines is finally achieved.

Unless single notes can be found without hesitation, it is of little use to attempt to read anything containing double notes or chords. In each of these three aspects of note-reading the primary need of establishing the key centre before attempting anything is all important.

Accidentals and ledger lines should be observed and named before beginning any exercise.

Because knowledge of harmony plays a major note in sight-reading, we must learn to think and read from the bass upwards. The immediate recognition of intervals and chords, whether the notes are played simultaneously or in arpeggio, often requires much laborious training. Usually the study of simple chords and progressions is left much too late in a pupil's development. It cannot be sufficiently stressed that this branch of our work should begin really early. This makes chord

H

recognition much easier. (The musicianship examinations set by the Associated Board Grades IV–VII can greatly help in stimulating interest in chord progression and recognition.) The finding of note groups on the keyboard should be developed by the 'feel' of the black and white note position. The process is the same as that used by anyone who is blind.

To begin with all time values must be read as if on a monotone. The time patterns should be tapped out in one hand while the other hand taps the beats only. This is a difficult process to learn, but the control which results will repay all the trouble taken. Daily practice along these lines will pay dividends. Every piece can be treated as a sight-reading exercise. The two processes of (a) note-reading and finding and (b) of tapping out the time patterns at a given pulsation must be dealt with separately before being attempted in combination.

As the sounds are made in time, the melodic and harmonic features of the phrases will gradually be realised and constructive treatment of the music will become possible. The stage of development of our musical instinct and mental training naturally qualifies all we do.

Encourage your pupil to sight-read anything he or she can lay hands on.

Pop music is excellent for rhythmic training and at certain stages can be a great stimulus for this subject of 'sight-reading'. If we have done our job rightly, this will do nothing to disturb our pupil's taste and love for the best in music. If possible, have a session weekly of playing duets with a similarly graded fellow student. In this way knowledge is built up of the orchestral repertoire, much of which is arranged for this combination. Pupils soon realise the great advantage of being a 'good reader'.

Above all, of course, is the golden rule to look ahead and keep going. This process can be compared to driving a car, where many physical processes have to be carried out at one and the same time. In fact, we can point out, each piece of reading is passing through a musical landscape, no detail of which escapes us.

9
Pros and Cons

Parents and others who are responsible for encouraging young people to take up music, with the idea of earning a reasonable living, would do well to ponder over the pros and cons.

As far as the piano is concerned it is very difficult, but not by any means impossible, to make a living as a soloist.

In these days of government grants and, of course, help from institutions, young pianists have more aid than ever before to come before the public. Experience as a soloist no doubt makes us able to teach to a higher standard and entitles us to higher fees.

It is a great mistake for anyone to be encouraged to make music a profession, unless there is real talent and a first-class brain. Gone are the days when the music profession was the last resort of those of us who were no good at anything else. The profession is still suffering from this outlook which unfortunately is still not uncommon.

If there is real talent, however, as teachers we must fight hard for our students to have extra time for practice. In this country the decision is invariably taken far too late in school days for an adequate teaching to be attained. Technical requirements are very high nowadays and the foundations must be laid early in life. In our present system of education there must always be a war between the academic studies and learning an instrument, as homework encroaches upon practice time. The Music Schools at present opening throughout the country are, certainly, one answer to the problem and the Saturday morning schemes for musical training held by the colleges do, at any rate, see that no real talent need be wasted.

The musical boy or girl in school also takes the GCE and 'A' level music. However, nothing makes up for the actual hours of piano practice which are so necessary to build up a repertoire which will go through life with us. Whether we teach in school or privately, we must always try to arrange extra practice from pupils and, if necessary, stand up to the heads of schools and gain our point.

In the light of what has been said above, we must ask ourselves what is the role of the private music teacher in this very puzzling educational mêlée. It is indeed sad that there has to be a struggle between general education and the specialist in music. Society needs artists as never before.

There is, of course, a role for the private teacher in our society, Many parents like their children to learn piano in a different atmosphere from that of the place where they receive their general education, and there is no doubt that the music studio can be a very attractive place which will stimulate the interest of the young in the art of playing an instrument.

Teachers should strive to have the best equipment available, with two pianos if possible. This is an item for which one should pay for the very best that can be afforded. A good library of music and text-books should be built up as time goes on. The covering and care of these should be stressed. No dirty hands please! The attractive use of colour schemes and pictures in the studio itself can stimulate a love of the beautiful and best, cultivate taste and be an excellent background for study. Make your studio a place that people love to visit.

A tape recorder is a useful piece of equipment, and a playback of pieces at various stages of development can be a very real help.

Many young teachers find the settling of the correct fees a vexed question. This, of course, is bound up with the type of town or suburb in which we live. Outside London fees are undoubtedly lower, and some districts have a larger proportion of professional and prosperous residents. Here higher fees can be charged. Much helpful advice can be obtained from the Music Teachers Association, 106 Gloucester Place, W.I., and the Incorporated Society of Musicians Ltd., 48, Gloucester Place, W.I. Never, never vary fees. Good relationships are impossible if this is done. Parents talk!

In the foregoing paragraphs little has been said of the teacher's equipment other than good training. No other profession perhaps needs such a reserve of character and an ability to understand and have patience, with the not so bright student. An ability to 'jolly along' Heads of Schools and have good relations with our colleagues is a talent too little cultivated by many of us. Perhaps this aspect of our work is not sufficiently stressed. The most splendid training is useless if character and an enthusiastic personality are lacking. When a good and sound private connection is being built up pupils' concerts can be of great help. Perhaps two a year (Christmas and Midsummer) at which the earliest beginner can make a small contribution as a partner (say) in an easy duet. Light refreshments help the atmosphere to become homely, and informal, and much propaganda work can be done on these occasions.

From the outset help your students to have a sincere and a professional approach to performance. Deportment on the concert platform and courtesy to fellow students should be stressed—no talking whilst others perform is a strict rule!

Rehearsals for concerts should be held beforehand, and no student below a certain standard should be allowed to perform at the concert itself, i.e. they must *know* their work whether simple or difficult. In this way standards are raised, in a quite remarkable way. The stronger help the weaker. Encourage parents to attend these rehearsals. Never, never omit *praise* and *encouragement* if even the slightest effort has been made to improve.

Musical Festivals can also be of great assistance to raising standards. These affairs show up mercilessly the difference between good and bad teaching. These are some of the ways we can make our profession more highly respected, and of real service to the community in which we live, and this surely is the aim of all 'We Piano Teachers'.

Appendix

Musical Sense Allied to Possible Effects in Performance

Note outline for the lecture delivered by Victor Booth at the Duke's Hall, Royal Academy of Music, on 21st March 1927.

I feel the double title I have chosen for this lecture requires some explanation. By musical *Sense* I mean something *different* from musical *Expression*. I imagine that *sense* in Music is dependent upon our logical faculties; and that *Expression* (or aptness in effect) can be judged only by our so-called musical instinct. It seems to me quite possible to be *sensible* in performing music without being in the least *expressive*, but any attempt at being *expressive* without this necessary basis of *sense* is bound to produce an unsatisfactory result.

I believe that *expression in speech and music* is strikingly similar in many respects.

Take, for example, the average school child reciting a little poem; she pronounces the words correctly and with more or less the necessary metrical accentuation:

'The boy stood on the burning deck' etc.

This sort of effort may be quite sensible but could scarcely be called even remotely *expressive*.

To take a more dramatic example I am very fond of quoting to my own pupils, which shows up the vast difference between mere sense and an expressive reading:

'Out of the night that covers me' etc.

Without attempting to encroach on Mr Acton Bond's preserves, I presume if he wanted an expressive reading of such a poem he would go to some considerable trouble to explain things, possibly pointing out the necessity for underlining certain words and keeping others in the background, how to employ definite intonations and cadences of the voice and so on, in order that the inner meaning of the poem might be immediately perceived by the listener.

It is quite possible to get perhaps several different yet entirely satisfactory readings of the same poem, and the same possibility often prevails in interpreting a piece of music. There can surely never be only one right way as regards details. The question of emphasis and the underlining of various points will naturally strike different people in different ways, but the broad basis of pronunciation, punctuation and sense must always remain the same. (Follow with a musical analogy.)

Now surely what happens in getting at the sense of a poem also happens with regard to music. Let us take a small piece of Schumann's 'Träumerei'. Many children would play this quite accurately as regards notes, etc., and more or less 'in time' as we say; some would even play it metrically correctly, and still it misses fire musically.

Possibly something like this. *Give example.*

[*Träumerei.* Victor Booth loved the music of Schumann and the Romantic School. He would have pointed out in this example that this apparently simple piece is extraordinarily difficult to play. Each phrase opens with a rise of a fourth, the second unit rising to the second beat of the second bar, then spreading away into clustering harmonies reflecting the wandering dreams of the poet and musician —Schumann himself. A. F.]

My experience is that teachers very often are at their wits' end to know what to do to improve matters. Now, surely, if they treated this piece in many respects as a poem ought to be treated, pointing out the similarities and differences between the phrases, the necessity for underlining certain beats because of this or that relationship, and the still greater necessity for keeping others in the background, they would be getting well on the road to a more satisfactory interpretation. Perhaps I had better explain what I mean. Let us take *the similarities* in this piece. *Give example.*

I don't wish, at this point in the lecture, to deal in the least exhaustively with these possibilities, or I shall anticipate too much of what I want to say later on.

Now I think we interpreters of music can probably learn more by noticing what is wrong rather than what is right in speech. Take the question of metre again. Would any child be guilty of this sort of thing?

>   >   >   >
'The boy stood on the burning deck' or
> >   >   >
'Out of the night that covers me'.

And yet, alas! how often one hears this done in music, even by would-be Licentiates of the R.A.M. One listens in amazement to this sort of accentuation. *Give example.*

[The examples given here by Victor Booth undoubtedly refer to the subjects of Fugues No. 16 in G minor and No. 21 in B♭ major. (Book I *Forty-eight Preludes and Fugues* J. S. Bach.) How often do we hear these subjects played with undue accentuation on the first note, which is a weak beat! A.F.]

One must remember that even in *shouting* the weak syllables still remain relatively weak. However loudly you shout it is never *The Royal Academy of Music*. And in playing double forte phrases in music one must remember this fact just as surely. Some people attribute these *badnesses* to either faults in technique or listening, but I am strongly of opinion that the right fundamental point of view is wanting. Wrong imagination, if you like.

Take correct and incorrect pronunciation in speech—what we call accent in music. If you said to anyone 'Come and see me to-morrow', they would certainly have to think twice before they knew what you were talking about. And yet in music how often do we get again and again 'to-morrow' and 'to-day' for 'to-morrow' and 'to-day'.

Take the well-known example on the first page of the Beethoven C minor Sonata, Op. 10, No. 1.

Give example:

Up to the present I have quoted very simple effects which, of course, are obvious to everyone, but when one attempts to apply to musical performance what is effective in dramatic speech one is called upon to observe closely just what happens under these conditions.

Now, apart from tonal emphasis, this surely introduces us to two very potent factors for musical effect, and to give them in simple terms might we not call them the hesitating and leaning accents? One could fill volumes with examples of these effects. (C minor Example Beethoven.) We all know the look of Sir Henry Wood when he has been piling phrase upon phrase and suddenly the stick is poised in the air before that final accent which clinches the musical argument. And don't we also all know the orator who almost lifts us out of our seat with a similar effect? 'He would do this and that and so on and so on *and*—didn't I tell you so?'

I trust that what I have said up to now will serve to explain roughly *why* I chose the double title of 'Musical Sense allied to possible effects in performance'. Now I would like to say something about actually what is *music*, and why it makes its appeal so universally.

I will try to convince you that music is not only useful for the gratification it gives during performance but that in its essence, as

I

a language of the feelings, it has a very definite influence in the formation of the national character.

'Man judges according to his feelings even in the construction of religious conceptions.'

If that is so, and if what I am about to say proves convincing, this surely should be one of the strongest arguments in favour of the support and development in this country, not only of music generally, but of British music most particularly. Let us take the well-known quotation:

> The man that hath no music in himself,
> Nor is not moved with concord of sweet sounds,
> Is fit for treasons, stratagems, and spoils;
> The motions of his spirit are dull as night
> And his affections are dark as Erebus:
> Let no such man be trusted.'

In writing thus Shakespeare may have been rather hard on the unmusical soul but at any rate he seems to have been quite convinced that the musical one had at least the possibilities of virtue and right-mindedness. And I fancy he never intended that these virtues belong exclusively to any particular nation.

One of our greatest psychologists and perhaps the greatest authority on education, Herbert Spencer, has left a quite remarkable essay on 'The Origin and Function of Music'. I quote him in preference to others, as it is most unlikely that he had any axe to grind in the cause of music in particular.

He regarded it not only as 'The highest of the Fine Arts' but also, 'The one which, more than any other, ministers to the human welfare'. He explains this by saying:

'Just as there has silently grown up a language of ideas, which, rude as it first was, now enables us to convey with precision the most subtle and complicated thoughts; so there is still silently growing up a *language of feelings* which, notwithstanding its present imperfection, we may expect will ultimately enable men vividly and completely to impress on each other all the emotions which they experience from moment to moment.'

And again he says:

'In its bearing upon human happiness, we believe that *this emotional language which musical culture develops and refines* is only second in importance to the language of the intellect, perhaps not even second to it.... Leaving out of view the immediate gratifications it (music) is hourly giving, we cannot too much applaud that progress of musical culture which is becoming one of the characteristics of our age.'

These quotations seem to me quite adequate enough without going further afield, and dispense surely with the necessity for any apology, because the study of music *has* become so much more general.

Spencer, who is largely responsible for the modern educational system all over the world with the great guiding principles of 'independent observation' and 'self-instruction', gives us his definition of what music actually *is*. He says:

'Music is but the idealisation of the natural language of emotion.' That: 'The various inflections of voice which accompany feelings of different kinds and intensities are the germs out of which music is developed.' And further: 'It is demonstrable that these inflections and cadences are not accidental or arbitrary but that they are determined by certain general principles of vital action, and their expressiveness depends on this.'

I am not here to argue the pros and cons of these statements, but I want to tell you how they appeal to me personally.

The substance of his essay, put conversationally, seems to be this: that we can tell the sentiment of any speech expressively spoken, even without hearing the actual words or even understanding them, merely from the rise and fall of the voice, the variation in tone, the general rate and variation of speed, of speaking. That *terror, horror; excitement, tranquillity; passion, grief, joy* and so on, all necessitate a definite method of delivery to convey their meaning. That *all* sounds and movements heard and seen in everyday life, below and above the normally expected, produce some effect, which will vary in accordance with the susceptibility of the individuals concerned.

Now here surely we have some real material upon which to model our musical moods. We all know how difficult it is to say the right thing in the right way even in our conventional relationships, but to do it at the more emotional crises of our lives is infinitely more difficult.

If it is a sin against human taste to clap a fellow on the back and say cheerfully: 'Jolly hard luck your losing your father, old chap', what are we going to say to similar offenders against musical taste?

Take the slow movement of the D major Sonata of Beethoven, Op. 10, No. 3. *Example*: Played too quickly.

The composer has marked this *largo e mesto*. Now I want to make one or two points clear as to how to deal with these terms. *Largo*, we know, means slowly, in a dignified style, and *mesto*, sadly. That is what we get in the dictionary, and this is just where a great many students stop short, but surely this mere knowledge that these terms mean slowly and sadly must be applied and in such a way that we re-create this particular character, sentiment or idea of Beethoven's. Now the only way we can do it satisfactorily is through the imagination and the only invariable standard of reference we have to go upon lies with our impressions of the various sounds and movements that have surrounded us during our everyday lives.

How does a man move to suggest the idea of dignity? How does he speak to express the idea of sadness? Now, the two points I want to drive home are just these. First, that it is not enough merely to notice and understand terms and symbols, but that we must also imagine the facts they express. Secondly, that we must have some practical method for stimulating the imagination and that there is reason in adopting something more or less on the lines I have just suggested.

Having imagined and meditated upon a piece in this way, everything we do in performance will have reference to this fundamental movement. If we return to our Beethoven Sonata by a process of elimination, trying it one way and then another, it ought not to take us very long to make up our minds which is the most fitting and likely to produce the effect we earnestly desire.

That is a very important point. We must always earnestly desire a certain result and of course listen with all our senses alert to achieve it. Now, we tried the opening bars of this movement in a way so far removed from the composer's intentions that of course it was quite unfitting. Now let us try it in a different way.

Example: Play rather emotionally (rubato).

Our question is the simple one, Is this result in accordance with our ideas of producing an effect of dignified sadness? If we think so, then our instinct for fitness or aptness in effect must be a very poor affair indeed. It surely couldn't take us long to arrive at the conviction that something like this is more what we really want.

Last example: The D. minor movement.

This question of fitness for the mood or character of a piece is an all-important one. If you were asked to play the part of a Duke, etc., or of a waiter, etc.

Now some composers give very clear indications of what they want, as, for instance, Beethoven in the above example. Others give only a *tempo* mark, such as *allegro, moderato* and suchlike. In these cases you have to get your mood very largely from the general rate of movement, aided, of course, by the nature of the piece in question. I had a pupil many years ago who was very fond of playing in a very expressive manner. You know the sort of thing. She produced her piece somewhat like this:

Example: Mendelssohn *Lieder ohne Worte, No. 14.*

[Mendelssohn was certainly one of Victor Booth's favourite composers and considered by him to be unjustly neglected as far as keyboard compositions are concerned. A.F.]

She had, of course, completely disregarded the composer's tempo indication, which was, I think, *allegro moderato*. When I suggested it might perhaps go somewhat like this she was quite shocked and no doubt thought me a very unmusical person.

Example: (*Allegro moderato*).

Possibly she was at that wonderful stage in life when everything must wear the garb of romance. Many people offend against musical taste by trying to unload this precious article on every possible occasion. We often get L.R.A.M. candidates who give a performance something like this:

Example: Sonata in A♭ Op. 26 (Air and Variations).

I am afraid examiners are rather prone to regard this sort of thing more as a type of musical gush which is bound to offend instead of making the desired musical impression.

Before leaving this question of aptness in effect let us take one or two more examples. They are both from Chopin. The first Prelude in C major is often given a quite different reading from the composer's intention, if we imagine the necessary treatment to produce the effect of *molto agitato*, which is the composer's mark.

Example: Played in two ways.

About the F. Major prelude there must be a good deal of licence in its treatment for the only indications are *moderato* and *pp*. There seems to be a quiet beauty pervading this piece and one must take care not to disturb this atmosphere by anything in the nature of an *agitato* movement.

Now let us look at what we have got on the written page of any piece of music. The composer supplies us with notes, rests, pitch, harmony and time values of various lengths, and merely suggestions for everything else, such as tempo, tone and so on.

If we agree that music is a language and as such must be regarded as a medium to present ideas, we must be prepared to subject it to some similar system of grouping as that applied to everyday speech before we are in a position to comprehend it logically. Don't forget we are talking about the interpreter as a performer. The listener is, of course, in a quite different category. You go to see and listen to a play and everything has been done for you, but just think of the enormous pains taken by everyone concerned in the presentation of that play. Now, given a piece of music to interpret, what sort of legacy does the composer leave us? Remember, the eye is the only medium between him and ourselves. Here we are with really little else but pages of syllables and suggestions. Now what would we do if we were asked to read a poem under similar conditions? Wouldn't we say that this was impossible until we had joined the syllables into words, the words into phrases and sentences, punctuated the whole thing in fact, and observed our capital letters and our rhymes. And even then we should only be in a position to read the thing sensibly. We should still have to do our close studies in the relations of this and that in order to be expressive and to make our delivery effective.

My plea is that many people who find it impossible to work alone at musical interpretation could do so quite successfully if they would only take the trouble to follow this plan of first finding and comparing the groups before attempting to combine them into performance. Granted that there are people of experience and blessed with a first-class musical instinct who seem to hit the nail on the head almost the very first time, yet they by their very facile methods will very often fail in effect, especially when dealing with abstruse works.

All the great authorities tell us the same thing about musical interpretation. They are agreed that this can only be achieved by a close study of the structure of every piece of music we wish to perform. If we had time I could quote Riemann, the German, Lussy, the Frenchman, Muggelini, the Italian, and our own principal, Dr McEwen. You would be very surprised at the amazing similarity in their statements.

This study of musical structure raises an interesting point. Our teachers of theory teach and explain music chiefly from the point of view of analysis, pulling the musical house to pieces, so to speak. This admittedly is essential, but the teacher of interpretation has a totally different task. Having observed and compared all the sections, he is then called upon to re-build the musical structure, and he has to be very careful not to put his roof where the floor ought to be. In other words, his climaxes must be arranged in a very definite relationship. You probably all know the very common fault in making a crescendo is to begin too loudly and vice versa with a diminuendo. This is really an elementary instance of anticipating your effects.

It is one thing to perform a piece of music under the guidance of some helping hand. It is quite another thing to do so alone and unaided. Yet this is usually the great problem that faces every student who is turned loose upon the world either as teacher or performer. I don't think I ever appreciated the enormous help

I had received from my teachers until I tried to work things out on my own account. Unfortunately, most of our so-called study is merely borrowed. It all seems so easy if you can go to someone and say, 'How does this go, what can I do here', and such like. But you get many a nasty knock when you must take only your own opinion for better or worse, and stand or fall by it. It was this necessity that made me realise when I left the Academy that strictly speaking our musical education only begins when we begin to educate ourselves, that we are faced with the fact that we must find some method of work and some system of thought to enable us to develop our own individuality.

The pianist's life is a very difficult one and must be regarded from a similar standpoint to that of the actor on the stage. Yet the task is much more difficult, for this reason. An actor plays only one part, whereas the pianist plays them all. The entire drama, so to speak, falls upon his shoulders alone. In a piece such as a sonata, each subject might be likened to a different character on the stage. The pianist plays the hero, heroine and the entire family. In a fugue he must be a complete trio, quartet and so on; it is just as necessary for his viola part to be worked up independently as his first violin, and then they all of them have to be combined and speak at once.

I have carefully refrained from discussing any effects in performance peculiar to the pianoforte as an instrument as I felt this was not within the scope of the present subject, but there is one effect that might be said to overlap, and that is what is commonly called tone balance, the giving of more tone to one or more parts than to others. This might be likened to the central placing of figures among many on the stage, so I feel justified in mentioning it here. There is no doubt whatever that this effect must be understood in all its possibilities if we ever hope to give a first-class performance. Just listen to an ordinary scale in double notes.

Example: Play in different ways.

Another example: Opening of G♭ study Op. 10 Chopin.

[Here again accentuation on the third beat of the bar instead of the first is a common fault. A.F.]

I had hoped to say a good deal on the rhythmic side of interpretation, but unfortunately there isn't time. One thing I must say before finishing and that is that much the most important element for effect in music is this rhythmic one. The shaping of musical statements through that elusive sensation of energy running in and energy running out, and always within the limits of sense, as suggested by the musical structure. Whatever else you do in performance, if this is absent your effects are bound to misfire.

To sum up: our aim and object must always be to be *sincere*; to re-create music with all our heart and mind, and with all respect and reverence for the intentions of the composer. This can only be accomplished by first following the dictates of reason; a careful observance of all groups and their logical succession and relationships; of all terms and symbols; and an earnest endeavour first to imagine our effects before attempting performance. We must explore all possible channels for effect, strictly in accordance with the sentiment, mood or character of the piece, before finally deciding that our ultimate endeavour is what we really intend. When remembering the enormous pains taken for every creation in the realms of art, surely we cannot expect to re-create without giving of our very best efforts too.

After what I have said to-day, you may or may not agree with me, but I believe there is a technique for musical expression. I believe it to be primarily a technique of musical thought or imagining, which in its elementary stages can be reduced to very few principles and so constitute a basis for musical sense. I also believe that the acquisition of this sense and the power of musical expression can be greatly aided and stimulated by an appreciation of music as a language, which, as such, follows the ordinary laws of reason, and that many possible effects in speech, more especially as illustrated in the forms of poetry and drama, may equally be used in the presentation of Music.

Bibliography

Among the most vital needs of the teacher, and an excellent aid to maintaining confidence and morale in a profession in which the practitioner often works in greater comparative isolation than teachers of most other subjects, is a well-filled bookshelf. Its contents should not be entirely limited to works originating in the United Kingdom, but attention should be paid to developments abroad. For example, American methods of approach in teaching piano to the very young well repay study, as in the works by Leila Fletcher and Edna May Burnam listed below. An easy way of keeping 'in touch' is to make sure that one's name is on the mailing lists of the leading music publishers, and to subscribe to at least one music journal, e.g. *The Music Teacher, Music and Musicians,* and *Music in Education,* not forgetting to watch for the occasional excellent articles in this field in *The Times Educational Supplement.* One must then ensure that one really does make time to read it with a notebook ready to jot down useful items and details of new books for wider reading.

It is taken for granted that the foundation of a library will be a good musical dictionary such as Groves (a new edition of which is now in preparation) and the invaluable *Oxford Companion to Music* of Dr Percy Scholes. (Add Mrs Curwen's *Teacher's Guide.*)

Among more recent publications, the following short list may be helpful:

The Young Pianist *Interpretation for the Piano Student* }	Joan Last	O.U.P.
Literature of the Piano (This is valuable as a reference work)	Ernest Hutcheson	Hutchinson 1950, 2nd revised edition 1969
Better Beginnings *Piano Playing* }	J. Ching	Bosworth
What Matthay Meant	A. Coviello	Bosworth

Biographies of composers are also essential for background knowledge, and your local librarian will be pleased to advise on the latest books in this field as well as on older and well-tested publications.

It cannot be stressed too much that teaching methods should never slavishly follow any text book by anyone, however exalted!

Read—ponder—and make your own method, is the best advice to young teachers. Everyone has something unique to offer their profession! Have faith in your own ideas.

In the following lists of suggested primers and following up publications, I have concentrated more on study for the technique of modern works, the classical and romantic repertoire having been already dealt with in the chapter on repertoire.

Primers

Off we go *Off we go again*	} Diller-Quaile	Chappell
Making Music (Books 1 and 2)	Blake & Capp	Boosey & Hawkes
The Way Ahead (Books 1 and 2)	Mary Donnington	Assoc. Board
First Album (Books 1–3)	Christine Brown	Freemann
At the Keyboard (Books 1–4)	Joan Last	O.U.P.
The Young Pianist's *Repertoire*	Fanny Waterman and Marian Harewood	Faber Music Ltd.

Excellent teaching material to follow up may be found in:

Dimitri Kabalevsky (Grades 1–8)	Boosey & Hawkes
Felix Swinstead (Grades 1–8)	Associated Board
Hundred Best Short Classics (Books 1–7)	Paterson's Publications
Leslie Fly	Forsyth
Cyril Dalmaine	Forsyth
Malcolm Williamson	Chappell

For the teaching and preparation for modern techniques:

Travel Diaries (Five books)	Malcolm Williamson	Chappell	
Jardin d'Enfants (Books 1 and 2) *Pièces Ingénues*	} Collection Alpha.	J. Clergue	Lemoine & Cie

(*Jardin d'Enfants* is a collection of modern French pieces for children, and is a splendid foundation for the study of C. Debussy.)

Wir Bauen Eine Stadt	Hindemith	Schott
Mikrokosmos (Books 1–6)	B. Bártók	Boosey & Hawkes
Pieces for Children (Books 1 and 2)	B. Bártók	Boosey & Hawkes

Aids to Reading at Sight

Rhythmic Reading	Joan Last	O.U.P.
(Books 1–5)		
Sight Reading	Mrs. Curwen	Curwen
(Books 1 and 2)		
(Book 2 out of print)		
Play at Sight	Christine Brown	Freeman
(Books 1–4)		

For finger agility and technique

A Dozen a Day	Edna M. Burham	Schirmer
(Books 1–5)		
Exercises Préparatoires	A Schmitt	(Many editions)
Hanon-Plaidy		Schirmer
(finger exercises)		
O. Beringer		Bosworth
(finger exercises)		
Pianist's Warming up	Harold Bauer	Chappell
Exercises		

For the more Advanced Student

Fifty-one Exercises	J. Brahms	Schirmer
Exercises de Tenues	I. Philipp	U.M.P.

(All Philipp's technical books are first class)

Introduction to Writing Work
(Theory of Music)

Fletcher Theory Papers	L. Fletcher	Schirmer
(Sets 1–3)		

(These elementary theory papers present this subject most attractively to the very young and are a good preparation for the Associated Board publications which can be used later.)

This short list of music and test books makes no claim to be comprehensive. As before stated teachers must find their own methods of presentation. In any case too long lists tend to be bewildering rather than helpful. Great care should be exerised in choice of editions. These vary enormously—for example, nothing could be better than the Henle Urtext editions of the keyboard works of Bach (although the Goldberg Variations* are omitted) and Mozart. You will no no doubt find your favourite pieces as well as the old and tried ones. Good luck! and good pupils and above all good teaching. A.F.

*Ralph Kirkpatrick's Schirmer edition of these Variations is recommended. A.F.

Index